curry

curry

A Global History

Colleen Taylor Sen

SPEAKING TIGER

SPEAKING TIGER PUBLISHING PVT. LTD
4381/4, Ansari Road, Daryaganj,
New Delhi–110002, India

Curry: A Global History by Colleen Taylor Sen was first published by Reaktion Books in the Edible series, London, UK, 2009

First published in India by Speaking Tiger in paperback 2017

For sale in South Asia only

ISBN: 978-93-86338-83-9

10 9 8 7 6 5 4 3 2 1

Printed at Gopsons Papers Ltd.

Contents

Introduction: What is Curry?

> No source of influence in cookery . . . has exceeded imperialism. . . . The tides of empire run in two directions: first, the flow outward from an imperial center creates metropolitan diversity and 'frontier' cultures – cuisines of miscegenation – at the edges of empires. Then the ebb of imperial retreat carries home colonists with exotically acclimatized palates and releases the forces of counter-colonization, dappling the former imperial heartlands with enclaves of sometimes subject peoples, who carry their cuisine with them.
>
> Felipe Fernández-Armesto, *Near a Thousand Tables: A History of Food* (New York, 2002)

If any dish deserves to be called global, it is curry. From Newfoundland to the Antarctic, from Beijing to Warsaw,[1] there is scarcely a place where curries are not enjoyed.

But what is a curry? The definition of the word is elusive and controversial. In this book, we define curry the following way: a curry is a spiced meat, fish or vegetable stew served with rice, bread, cornmeal or another starch. The spices may be freshly prepared as a powder or a spice paste or purchased as a ready-made mixture.

The extensive use of spices is the most characteristic feature of Indian cuisine.

This very broad definition is an umbrella for many dishes: the classic Anglo-Indian curries of the Raj; the elegant *gaengs* of Thailand; the exuberant curries of the Caribbean; *kari raisu*, Japan's favourite comfort food; Indonesian *gulais*; Malaysia's delicious *Nonya* cuisine; South African bunny chow and bobotie; Mauritian *vindaille*; and Singapore's fiery street foods. The story of these and other dishes will be told in the following chapters.

A secondary definition of curry is any dish, wet or dry, flavoured with curry powder – a ready-made mixture that generally includes turmeric, cumin seed, coriander seed, chillies and fenugreek[2] (and may or may not include curry leaf, *Murraya koenigii*, a fragrant leaf widely used in southern Indian cooking). This category encompasses such diverse, hybrid dishes as German *currywurst*, Singapore noodles, Dutch fries with curry ketchup and American curried chicken salad.

Although there are many fanciful – and sometimes hilarious – explanations of the origin of the word 'curry',[3] it probably derives from southern Indian languages, where *karil* or *kari* denoted a spiced dish of sautéed vegetables and meat. In the early seventeenth century, the Portuguese used the word *caril* or *caree* to describe broths 'made with Butter, the pulp of Indian nuts . . . and all sorts of spices, particularly Cardamoms and Ginger . . . besides herbs, fruits and a thousand other condiments . . . poured in good quantity . . . upon boiled Rice'.[4] In English, *caril* became curry, which Hobson-Jobson, the great dictionary of nineteenth-century

One of the traditional ways of grinding spices is in a mortar and pestle.

Curry leaves are used in many Indian dishes, although they are not a component of all curry powders.

British–Indian English, describes as 'meat, fish, fruit or vegetables, cooked with a quantity of bruised spices and turmeric, and a little of this give a flavour to a large mess of rice'.

Traditionally, the word 'curry' was not used by Indians, who called dishes by their specific names: *korma*, *rogan josh*, *molee*, *vindaloo*, *doh piaza*, etc. But today Indians often use the word for any home-made dish with a gravy, especially when talking with non-Indians. Even the celebrated Indian cookbook writer Madhur Jaffrey, who in 1974 wrote that the word 'curry' was 'as degrading to India's great cuisine as the term "chop suey" was to China's', called a later book *The Ultimate Curry Bible* (2003) – an indication of how the word has gained widespread currency.

Purists would insist that the only dish that deserves to be called curry is the one developed in the kitchens of British India in the late eighteenth century. This classic Anglo-Indian curry, which reached its apogee in the recipes of Colonel Kenney-Herbert (Wyvern), is made by sautéing onions in oil, adding pieces of meat or fish, and simmering it in water, stock, tomatoes or coconut milk. Spices – either freshly ground or a commercial curry powder – are added during the sautéing process.

These curries were always served with rice and various condiments such as peanuts, sliced or grated coconut, Bombay duck (dried Bomelo fish), sliced cucumbers and tomatoes, pickles and fruit chutneys. Initially a dish of the British upper classes, it gradually filtered down to middle-class and then to working-class tables. Curry lunches were a popular way of entertaining people in the '50s, '60s and even as late as the 1970s.

In the nineteenth century, a wide range of commercial curry powders made it easy for British housewives to prepare curries at home.

This style of curry was disseminated throughout the Empire by British cookbooks, immigrants and officials who, like modern executives, were transferred to different divisions of Great Britain, Inc. English-style curries became standard items in the taverns of nineteenth-century America, Canada, New Zealand and Australia (where a leading novelist once advocated making curry the national dish).

Curries and their cousins are an integral part of the cuisines of South-East Asia and Indonesia. As early as the third century BC, Indian traders and Buddhist missionaries brought tamarind, garlic, shallots, ginger, turmeric and pepper to the region. Starting from the eighth century AD, Arab traders introduced kabobs, biryanis, kormas and other meat dishes from others parts of the Islamic world, including the Middle East, Persia and India.

In the late fifteenth century, the Portuguese took over the spice trade and built a far-flung chain of trading posts in the Persian Gulf, the Malacca Straits, Indonesia, India and South

In 2004 the British Foreign Secretary proclaimed chicken tikka masala a 'true British national dish' because it exemplifies the multiculturalism of British society.

Africa. In what is called the 'Columbian exchange', these settlements became the hub of a global exchange of fruits, vegetables, nuts and other plants between the western hemisphere, Africa, Oceania and the Indian subcontinent. One of the most important of these plants was the chilli pepper, which was rapidly assimilated into many local cuisines and became an essential element in curries.

In the seventeenth century, Portugal lost much of its empire to the British and the Dutch. The British Empire eventually came to encompass India, Ceylon, Burma, Malaya and Singapore, Australia, New Zealand, most of North America, Trinidad, Guyana, Fiji, Mauritius and many parts of Africa. The Dutch gained control over Indonesia, Ceylon, Surinam, the Antilles and South Africa. An important event in the history of curry is the abolition of the slave trade in the British Empire in 1807, followed by the abolition of slavery in 1833. To replace the freed slaves, the British brought in more than a million indentured labourers from the Indian subcontinent to work on plantations in the West Indies, South Africa, Malaysia, Mauritius, Sri Lanka and Fiji. The new arrivals integrated local ingredients into their eating habits to create new varieties of curries. A similar phenomenon occurred in the Dutch colonies.

But the traffic has not been all one way. Even under colonial rule, there was a trickle of people, ingredients and dishes from the colonies to the motherland, which became a flood after they gained their independence following World War Two.

In modern Britain, curry is on the menus of thousands of restaurants and curry houses and nearly as many pubs, some of which have special 'curry nights'.

In The Hague, Amsterdam and other Dutch cities, many restaurants and shops sell Indonesian and Surinamese dishes and ingredients. Meanwhile, in New York and London, upmarket restaurants with Michelin stars serve sophisticated versions of curry using local ingredients, accompanied by elegant wines. Curry, the global dish par excellence, continues to evolve and adapt to changing times.

I

The Origins of Curry

First a sun, fierce and glaring, that scorches and bakes
Palankeens, perspiration and worry;
Mosquitoes, thugs, cocoa-nuts, Brahmins and snakes
With elephants, tigers and Curry.

Captain G. F. Atkinson, *Curry & Rice: The Ingredients of Social Life at 'Our Station' in India*, 1859

No other part of the world has the ethnic, linguistic, cultural, religious, climatic or culinary diversity of the Indian subcontinent.[1] The fertile plains of the Indus and Ganges rivers, the alluvial deltas of Bengal and the spice gardens of the Malabar Coast have yielded an agricultural bounty that was the foundation of a rich, varied cuisine. But most food is still produced and consumed regionally, and India has no national cuisine or national dish.

From prehistoric times, India's geographic location has made it a magnet for migrations and invasions. The newcomers brought ingredients, dishes and cooking techniques, making Indian cuisine the fusion food par excellence. But the exchange was not one way. India exported its spices and dishes to the rest of the world, including mangos, sugar cane, tea, mulligatawny soup, kedgeree and the subject of this book, curry.

The Subcontinent and its Food

Archaeological evidence indicates that the earliest inhabitants of the subcontinent subsisted on a diet of rice, barley, lentils, pumpkins, aubergines, bananas, coconut, citrus fruits, jackfruit and mangoes. They were the first people in the world to domesticate jungle fowl. Indigenous spices included turmeric, ginger, tamarind and long pepper (*Piper longum*).

Starting around 2000 BC, tribes of Indo-European pastoral semi-nomads migrated from the region between the Caspian and Black seas into northern India with their horses, cows, religion and languages. Their diet sounds far from appealing. Its staple was barley fried in butter, parched, ground into a meal mixed with yogurt, water or milk, or prepared as a gruel. Later they cultivated wheat, millet and rice. Dairy products, including yogurt and clarified butter, were widely consumed, as they are today. Their religious practices evolved into what is today called Hinduism and a caste system took shape.

The Indo-Europeans were not vegetarian and even ate beef. Around 500 BC two new religions emerged, Buddhism and Jainism, which preached non-violence and opposed the killing of animals for food. Vegetarianism became more common and austerity was associated with spirituality and high status. The tribes evolved into kingdoms and empires, and between 300 BC and AD 300, India was the wealthiest land in the world. Its merchants exported pepper, cardamom, silks and other luxury goods to the Roman Empire via Egypt. Caravans carried Indian goods over the Silk Road to the Persian Gulf, central Asia and China. Indian merchants sailed to South-East Asia, taking with them not only spices and textiles, but also Buddhism and Hinduism, art and dance forms, and Indian concepts of statecraft. The Chola dynasty based in

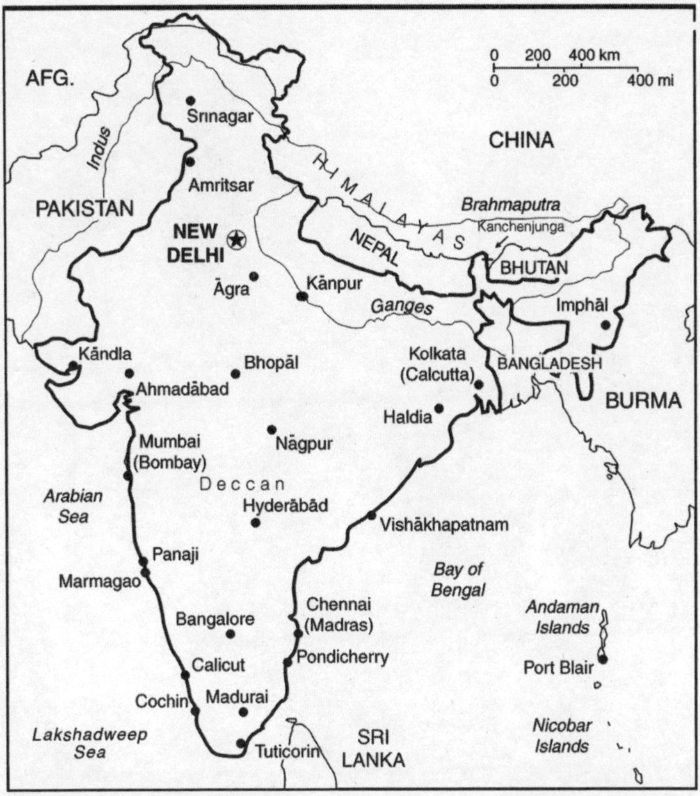

The Federal Republic of India consists of 29 states and 6 Union Territories. Some states are larger than most countries and have distinct languages, ethnicities, cultures and cuisines.

Tamil Nadu was a major maritime power with outposts in Ceylon, Java, Borneo, Sumatra and the Malaya Peninsula.

In the eighth century, Arab traders founded colonies on India's west coast. Islamic warriors from central Asia began to invade north-west India, initially to plunder its wealth, later to stay and rule. By the mid-thirteenth century, the Gangetic Valley was part of an Islamic sultanate with its capital near modern Delhi. For more than three hundred years, much of India was ruled by various Turkish, Afghan and central

An Indian cook prepares dishes in the traditional style.

Asian dynasties whose opulent courts attracted scholars and religious leaders from throughout the Islamic world.

These immigrants brought ingredients and dishes that today are misleadingly called 'Moghul' – a word that should be removed from the Indian culinary lexicon! From Persia came rosewater and saffron; from Afghanistan and central Asia, almonds, pistachios, raisins and dried fruit; from the Middle East, sweet dishes and pastries. They introduced sherbets and other sweetened drinks; *pulaos* and *biryanis*, elaborate dishes of rice and cooked meat; *samosa*, a meat- or vegetable-filled pastry; dozens of varieties of grilled and roasted meats called kabobs; *yakhni*, a meat broth; *dopiaza*, meat slowly cooked with onions; *korma*, meat marinated in yogurt and simmered over a slow fire; *khichri*, a blend of rice and lentils; *jalebi*, coils of batter deep-fried and soaked in sugar syrup; and nans and other baked breads.[2]

In this imaginative painting, four Moghul emperors, including Babur on the far left, and their courtiers enjoy a feast in a garden pavilion.

Many of these dishes have Persian names, which remained the language of culture in northern India until the nineteenth century. As one writer put it, 'To the somewhat austere Hindu dining ambience, the Muslims brought a refined and courtly etiquette of both group and individual dining. The Muslims influenced both the style and substance of Indian food.'[3] Meanwhile, the local cooks hired by the new rulers added their own spicing, creating a new Persian-Indian fusion cuisine.

In 1526 Babur, a descendant of the Mongol Genghis Khan, invaded northern India, defeated the ruler and proclaimed himself emperor of all Hindustan, thereby founding the Moghul dynasty (from the Persian word for Mongol). By 1700 the Moghuls had conquered the entire subcontinent except the very far south. In Europe, the word 'Moghul' was synonymous with fabulous power and wealth.

Abu'l Fazl 'Allami (1551–1602), prime minister of the emperor Akbar (Babur's grandson), has left a detailed record and description of the lavish kitchen at the royal court. He gives ingredients for 30 dishes that are still staples of north Indian cuisine. Although the lavish use of ghee (clarified butter) and spices such as cloves, cinnamon and cardamom epitomize the Moghuls' love of luxury and high living, most of the dishes were the same as those introduced by earlier Islamic rulers. (Babur even hired several cooks that had worked for the previous ruler of Delhi.) The imperial generals and noblemen, called nabobs or nawabs, had their own courts in Lahore, Hyderabad and Oudh (Lucknow), where they developed local variations of the imperial cuisine.

For centuries Europeans had sought a sea route to the Indian subcontinent. Spices were a great luxury, valued not only for their taste and medicinal properties but also as a way of showing off wealth. Until the fifteenth century, the spice trade had been controlled by Arab traders, but this trade was interrupted by the fall of Constantinople to the Turks in 1453. In 1498 the Portuguese explorer Vasco da Gama reached India's Malabar Coast. The Portuguese established a fortress on the island of Goa, Europe's first base on the Indian subcontinent (and the last to be relinquished, in 1961).

Goa was a key link in a chain of Portuguese forts and trading posts in the Persian Gulf, the Malacca Straits, Indonesia, India, Ceylon, Japan and South Africa. In what is called the 'Columbian exchange', the territories of the Portuguese and Spanish empires (Portugal united with Spain in 1580) became the hubs of a global exchange of fruits, vegetables, nuts and other plants between the western hemisphere, Africa, Oceania and the Indian subcontinent. The most important ingredient, and one essential to the story of curry, is the chilli pepper.

An 18th-century painting depicting a banquet at a royal court or aristocratic household.

Bombay was one of the three main ports of the East India Company.

On 31 December 1600 Queen Elizabeth I granted the East India Company, a group of English merchants, a monopoly of trade with the Indies. When the Dutch proved more powerful in the East Indies (Indonesia), the British turned their attention to India. The company built a chain of trading posts along both coasts and gradually extended their influence inland. In 1757 its troops defeated the Moghul forces and became the de facto rulers of large areas of India, although in theory they were subordinate to the British government.

In 1797 the British invaded Portuguese-ruled Goa, holding it for seventeen years before returning it to Portuguese rule. During this period, they discovered Goan cuisine, which combines classic Portuguese dishes, often made with beef and pork, with local ingredients. The most famous is vindaloo (from the Portuguese *vinha e alhos*, wine or wine vinegar and garlic) – a sour, fiery hot pork curry made with coconut vinegar, spices and red chillies. When the British left, they took these dishes and their Goan cooks with them.

By 1800 there were thousands of company administrators and military officers in India. They referred to themselves

In the eighteenth century, English men in India enjoyed lives of considerable luxury.

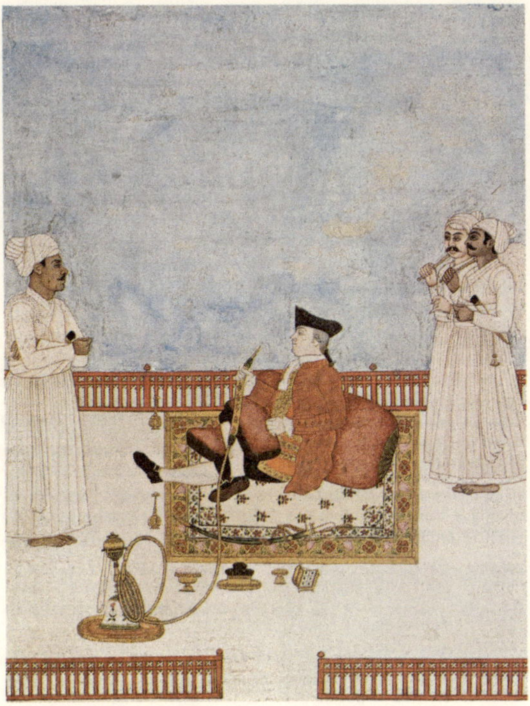

as 'Indians' or 'Anglo-Indians'. British India was divided into three presidencies, headquartered in Madras (Chennai), Bombay (Mumbai) and Calcutta (Kolkata). However, in 1833 the company lost its Indian trade monopoly. A revolt in 1857 (called the Indian Mutiny by British historians, and the First War of Independence by Indian writers) led to the end of Moghul rule and the transfer of power to the British government. In 1877 Queen Victoria was named 'Empress of India' and India officially became known as 'the Indian Empire'.

From this time until India gained its independence in 1947, around 60 per cent of its land area was under direct British rule. Both the territory and the administration are often referred to as the Raj. This territory included the three presidencies, the North-West Provinces, Punjab, Central

Provinces, Oudh (Lucknow) and British Burma. The so-called native states, ruled by local rulers, were in effect subordinate to the British government.

Indian Foods and Cooking Techniques

Until the end of the eighteenth century, there was little sense of racial superiority among the British, whose main motivation was profit. Company men lived much like the native population: they spoke Indian languages; took Indian mistresses and wives (often called 'sleeping dictionaries'); wore Indian clothes; and consumed Indian meals prepared by local cooks. Their heavy meat-centred meals featured spicy rice pulaos and biryanis, kabobs, kedgeree, chutneys, kormas, kalias and other Muslim dishes. The first British settlers may not have considered the highly spiced cuisine of India very strange, since in the early seventeenth century English cooking continued the tradition of the Middle Ages with its heavy use of cumin, caraway, ginger, pepper, cinnamon, cloves and nutmeg.

Then, as now, the food of the subcontinent was extremely diverse, reflecting regional, religious and social and caste differences, a discussion of which goes beyond the scope of this book. The basic techniques are deep frying, sautéing, boiling, braising and grilling. The most common cooking receptacle is a deep pot, *karahi* in Hindi, with two handles and a flat or slightly concave bottom.

A common Indian cooking technique with no exact equivalent in the West is called in Hindi *bhuna*. Spices and a paste of garlic, onions, ginger and sometimes tomatoes are fried in a little oil until they soften. Pieces of meat, fish or vegetables are sautéed in this mixture. Small amounts of water, yogurt or other liquid are then added a little at a time. The amount of liquid added and the cooking time determines whether the dish will be wet or dry. This is the basic technique used in making the dishes called curries.

The most distinctive feature of Indian cuisine is the use of spices and other strong flavourings, including garlic, onion and chillies. Many reasons have been given for the use of spices – and most are mythical. Hot spices do not induce enough perspiration to cool people down. Nor do they mask the flavour of tainted meat, since those who eat such food would be likely to die, or at the very least become seriously ill. The latest theory, backed by scientific evidence, is that a taste for spices evolved because they contain powerful antibiotic chemicals that kill or suppress the bacteria and fungi that spoil foods. The antibiotic effects are even stronger when combined with onions and garlic.

The gastronomical purpose of spices is to add flavour, texture and body to a dish. For the poor, they liven up simple dishes at low cost. Spices can be added in different ways and at different stages of the cooking process. At the start

A traditional way of preparing a meal in an Indian household.

of making a meat dish, whole spices are sautéed in ghee or oil to release their essential oils. Whole spices may be boiled with water, vegetables or meat and bones to make a stock. Spices may be ground into a wet paste with onions, garlic, ginger, yogurt, coconut milk, vinegar or some other liquid, sautéed and turned into gravy by the addition of liquid.

Spices may be ground into a powder and stored in airtight bottles for a couple of weeks. Often they are first dry roasted to bring out their aroma. In the process called tempering, whole or ground spices are sautéed in a little oil, sometimes with onions and garlic, and added to a dish when it has finished cooking to create additional bouquet.

In Hindi, a spice mixture is called a masala. Its ingredients depend on many factors, including regional preferences, religion and the other components of a dish. The use of cumin, coriander and chillies is nearly universal throughout the subcontinent. Hindus commonly add a pinch of turmeric to dals and vegetable dishes to impart flavour and colour. In Bengal, the basic spice mixture consists of cumin, black mustard seeds, nigella, fennel and fenugreek. Southern Indian vegetarian dishes are typically flavoured with coriander, cumin seeds, black pepper, mustard seeds, fenugreek, asafetida (a substitute for garlic among orthodox Hindus) and curry leaf. In north Indian cookery, a mixture called garam masala, or 'warm seasoning', made from cinnamon, cloves, cardamom and black pepper (but rarely turmeric) lends fragrance and aroma to meat dishes and is associated with Muslim cuisine.

The Rise of Curry . . .

By the late eighteenth century, the word 'curry' was in general use among the British. In his classic *Indian Domestic Economy and Receipt Book* (first published in 1841), Dr Robert Flower Riddell (*b.* 1798), the superintending army surgeon at the court of the Nizam of Hyderabad, describes curries in the following way:

> Curries consist in the meat, fish, or vegetables being first dressed [sautéed] until tender, to which are added ground spices, chillies, and salt to both the meat and gravy in certain proportions; which are served up dry or in the gravy; in fact, a curry may be made of almost any thing, its principal quality depending upon the spices being duly proportioned as to flavour and the degree of warmth to be given by the chillies and the ginger. The meat may be fried in butter, ghee, oil or fat, to which is added gravy, tyre [yogurt], milk, the juice of the coconut, or vegetables, etc.

Dr Riddell's recipes are for dishes made at the Nizam's court, including many for curry-like dishes called *salan*, a meat or vegetable dish with a thinnish gravy. He gives four recipes for curry powder which call for the same ingredients in different proportions: coriander seeds (roasted), turmeric (pounded), cumin seeds (dried and ground), fenugreek, mustard seed, dried ginger, black pepper, dried chillies, poppy seed, garlic, cardamom and cinnamon. A tablespoon of this mixture is recommended for a chicken curry together with six to twelve dried or green chillies(!) and one to three cloves of garlic. Tamarind, lime juice or mangoes, coconut milk or yogurt, and ginger can also be added.

A painting of nineteenth-century Indian cooks.

Another even more influential book published several decades later was *Culinary Jottings for Madras* (1878) written by Colonel Arthur Robert Kenney-Herbert (1840–1916) under the pen name Wyvern. Arriving in India in 1859 as a nineteen-year-old cadet, he was introduced to curries by a kind-hearted veteran, the last of a generation 'that fostered the art of curry-making and bestowed as much attention to it as we . . . do to copying the culinary triumphs of the lively Gauls'. This veteran held tiffin parties at which he would serve eight or nine curries accompanied by fresh chutneys, grilled ham, fish roe and other condiments. Guests were expected to taste each curry, discuss its merits and ask for second helpings of the ones they especially liked.

Kenney-Herbert, who was a great admirer and proponent of French cuisine, believed that a curry deserved the same care and attention as a classic French *fricassée* or *blanquette*. His elaborate and painstaking recipe for chicken curry remains a classic (but would strain the resources and skill of most modern cooks). He recommends that the curry powder be made at home in large batches and stored in tightly sealed glass bottles, and scorns people's lazy habit of allowing their cooks to make their 'curry stuff' on the spot as needed. But he does not oppose the use of ready-made curry powder and recommends Barrie's Madras Curry Powder and Paste (while warning against the curry powder sold by London grocers that is diluted with cornstarch and other contaminants).

His recipe (given on pp. 120–21) calls for the addition of small amounts of powdered cloves, mace, cinnamon, nutmeg, cardamom and allspice as well as 'judicious amounts' of green leaves of fennel, fenugreek, lemon grass, coriander and so on, or a paste of green ginger. An important element is a hint of sweet acid from tamarind and jaggery (unrefined brown sugar from palm sap). In England, acceptable substitutes are redcurrant jelly or chutney with a little vinegar or lime juice, or chopped apple and sour mango.

. . . and its Decline

By the middle of the nineteenth century, attitudes were starting to change, especially after the abolition of the East India Company in 1857 and the creation of the Imperial (later Indian) Civil Service in 1886. Britain continued to consolidate its territory possessions in India and with this came greater insulation from the people they ruled. The wearing of Indian clothes by Englishmen was banned, and the new public-school-educated officials looked down on the old company men who had 'gone native'.

The opening of the Suez Canal in 1869 made it easier and faster to ship goods and people to India. Indian wives and mistresses were replaced by British wives, many of whom had little formal or domestic education and were ill equipped to manage the small army of domestic servants that was standard. They avoided Indian cuisine in order to distance themselves from those they governed and to distinguish themselves from the old company men. Curries 'lost caste', as Kenney-Herbert put it, and were banished from fashionable tables, although they continued to be served in army mess halls, clubs and the homes of ordinary British civilians, especially at lunch.

Entertaining was an important part of social and professional life among British officials. At formal dinner parties guests were served 'tinned salmon, red-herrings, cheese, smoked sprats, raspberry jam, and dried fruits; these articles coming from Europe, and being sometimes very difficult to procure, are prized accordingly'.[4] Dishes with fancy French names became de rigueur.

To help the memsahibs cope with their new environment, old Indian hands wrote domestic handbooks with menus and recipes, most of them for British and European dishes. Recipes for Indian dishes were relegated to separate chapters and often referred to in derogatory terms. Flora Annie Steel, author of one of the most famous handbooks, writes that 'most native recipes are inordinately greasy and sweet'. The author of *The Indian Cookery Book* published in 1880 in Calcutta calls pellows (pulaos) 'purely Hindoostanee dishes', some of which are 'so entirely of an Asiatic character and taste that no European will ever be persuaded to partake of them'. Of korma, the author writes that it is 'one of the richest of Hindoostanee curries . . . but quite unsuited to European taste'.

The definition of what constituted a curry became more narrowly defined. The list of curries given in a typical nineteenth-century cookbook first published in 1891 (A Thirty-Five Years Resident, *The Indian Cookery Book: A Practical Handbook to the Kitchen in India adapted to the Three Presidencies*, Calcutta) is strikingly similar to the dishes on the

Dinner parties featuring roasts and imported dishes were an essential feature of British social life during the Raj.

Vindaloo (from the Portuguese dish *vinha de alhos*, or wine vinegar and garlic) is a hot and sour Goan dish traditionally made with pork. It is a staple of English curry houses.

menu of a twenty-first-century British curry house: doopiajas, gravy curries, kofta, hindostanee, hussanee, korma, malay, vindaloo, country captain, jhalfrezee, madras mulligatawny curry, chahkee, bhajees, dals and fish mooloos (molees). Some are not curries at all, but rather accompaniments to an Indian meal (see p. 33 for definitions).

Some writers have classified curries by city or region, such as Bengal, Madras, Bombay and Ceylon. But, as Lizzie Collingham points out, 'The Anglo-Indian understanding of regional differences was . . . rather blunt. They tended to hone in on distinctive but not necessarily ubiquitous, features of a region's cookery and then steadfastly apply these characteristics to every curry that came under that heading.'[5] Thus, all Ceylon curries were made with coconut milk, all Madras curries were hot, all kormas were made with yogurt, and so on.

The British had little familiarity with India's many other regional cuisines: the delicate vegetarian dishes of Gujarat and

Some Types of Indian Curry

Bhajee [bhaji]: a dry sautéed vegetable dish

Bhoona: a dry but tender curry made by slowly adding liquid to a dish as it is stir-fried

Ceylon curry: a hot creamy curry made with coconut milk

Country captain chicken: a simple dish, usually made with chicken

Dhansak: a mild, sweet and sour Parsi dish made with meat, lentils, and vegetables

Do(h)piaza: a curry made with a large proportion of onions

Hindoostanee: a north Indian curry that includes aromatic spices

Hussaini: meat threaded on skewers and cooked in a gravy

Jalfrezi: a stir-fried dish made with pre-cooked meat, onions, tomatoes and green peppers

Kalia (qalia): an aromatic preparation of fish, meat or vegetables with a sauce based on ground ginger and onion paste

Kofta: a meatball curry

Korma (qorma, qoorma): a mild aromatic braised whitish meat curry, made with yogurt, cream or coconut milk

Madras: a hot curry

Malay curry: a rich dish usually made with coconut milk

Molee, moolee, Malay: a curry, often made with fish, cooked in a thin coconut gravy

Pasanda: a curry made with long strips of meat

Patia: a mild sweet and sour Parsi fish curry

Phall: an extremely hot curry

Rogan josh: an aromatic meat dish marinated in yogurt and coloured red

Salan: a meat or vegetable dish with a thinnish gravy

Tikka masala: small pieces of meat, usually chicken, in a spicy, reddish-coloured gravy

Vindaloo: originally a hot and sour Portuguese-Indian pork dish; today code for a very hot curry.

Maharashtra, the complex seafood dishes of Kerala, the south India) or the pungent fish dishes of Bengal. There was a tendency to combine elements from different regions, by, for example, adding coconut milk, a standard ingredient in southern India, to north Indian Muslim dishes (equivalent, perhaps, to adding sesame oil to a coq au vin). Over time, curries became less authentic and more pan-Indian.

This homogenization was promoted by the constant movement of British officials. During their travels they stayed in *dak* (Hindi for post) bungalows – rest houses for travellers built every fifteen or twenty miles apart along main roads. The cooks would whip up a meal on the spot using whatever they could procure locally. One of the standards was country captain chicken, a dish that was to become very popular in the southern United States. See p. 121 for Dr Riddell's recipe.

At the same time, some British dishes became Indianized. Meat casseroles made with carrots and celery in a wine-based sauce were made more interesting by a dash of curry powder. Indian cooks minced left-over meat, coated it in mashed potatoes, egg and breadcrumbs, and fried it to make 'chops' or 'cutlets'. Indian-style omelettes, made with chillies and onions, are to this day a standard of Calcutta breakfasts.

A few Anglo-Indian hybrids became part and parcel of British cuisine. The breakfast dish kedgeree, a combination of rice, smoked fish, spices and hard-boiled eggs, is an elaboration of *khichri*, a simple mixture of boiled rice and lentils that is ubiquitous on the subcontinent. Another is mulligatawny soup, an adaption of southern Indian *rasam*, a thin broth of lentils, chillies and spices. The British added chicken, lamb or vegetables and thickened the liquid with flour and butter.

However, while curry 'lost caste' in India, the situation was very different in Britain, where all things Indian, from

Kashmiri shawls and Indian jewellery to curry, became the fashion among a new cosmopolitan middle class. By the end of the nineteenth century, curry had become thoroughly integrated into middle-class British cuisine.

2
Britain

Me and me mum and me dad and me gran
We're off to Waterloo,
Me and me mum and me dad and me gran
With a bucket of vindaloo.
Vindaloo, unofficial song of England
in the FIFA World Cup, 1998

One of the most remarkable developments in the history of gastronomy has been the emergence of curry as an archetypal British dish. It used to be axiomatic to equate British food with blandness, but 'going out for a curry', the hotter the better, has become a way of life for many urban Britons. More than eight thousand restaurants and curry houses and nearly as many pubs serve curry. Ready-made Indian meals are staples of supermarket and department stores, while packaged and frozen curries are sold throughout the British Isles. Curry has become the default take-away meal in the UK.

In 2001 a former foreign secretary, Robin Cook, proclaimed chicken tikka masala 'a true British national dish, not only because it is the most popular but because it is a perfect illustration of the way Britain absorbs and adapts external influences'.[1]

Why do Brits have an 'almost pathological affection' for Indian food? As Cook observed, it is a reflection of the multicultural nature of Britain and the availability of Indian dishes and ingredients. Immigration grew rapidly after World War Two and the partition of the Indian subcontinent in 1947, and many immigrants opened catering firms, small shops, importing businesses and restaurants throughout the British Isles.

Perhaps this affection, consciously or subconsciously, reflects nostalgia for the Raj and the days when Britannia ruled the waves, a nostalgia encouraged by the popularity of the television mini-series *Jewel in the Crown* in 1984. Some British families had historical ties with the subcontinent dating back to the eighteenth century. Finally, curry may be a welcome relief from the blandness of traditional British food and part of a global trend to explore 'hotter' and more exotic cuisines.

The Eighteenth and Nineteenth Centuries

By the end of the eighteenth century, company men, known as 'nawabs' or 'nabobs' because of their wealth, began returning home. Many lived in or near London. The 'Nabobery' was first located near Regent's Park and later in Bayswater and South Kensington. Just as the British tried to recreate their homeland while they were in India, now they tried to recapture something of their life in India after returning home.

Those who could afford it brought their cooks from India; others satisfied their appetite for curry at coffee houses. Curry was served in the Norris Street Coffee House at Haymarket in 1733. The first purely Indian restaurant was the

Hindoostanee Coffee House which opened in 1809 at 34 George Street near Portman Square, Mayfair. (Before it was torn down, the building was marked by a plaque.) Its proprietor was an interesting character named Sake Deen Mahomed (1759–1851), an Indian who had served in the British army and married an Irishwoman. He tried to provide both an authentic ambience and dishes 'allowed by the greatest epicures to be unequalled to any curries ever made in England'. However, the restaurant did not thrive and closed in 1833. One cause of its demise may have been the opening of the Oriental Club in 1824 in nearby Hanover Square as a meeting place for ex-company men. Its initial fare was French food; in 1839 it started serving curry. Today, the club continues the tradition by featuring a curry of the day on its menu.

William Makepeace Thackeray's *Vanity Fair* (1847–8) contains an amusing account of Becky Sharpe's dinner with the Sedleys at which she tries to snare the wealthy nabob, Josiah Sedley, the collector of Boggley Wollah, by feigning a love of

William Thackeray's *Vanity Fair* contains one of the first depictions of a wealthy India-returned 'nawab' in Josiah Sedley, depicted here with Becky Sharpe.

curry which she has never eaten, scorching her mouth in the process. Her surprise suggests that the dish remained relatively unknown outside Anglo-Indian circles in 1815 when the events of the novel took place.

The first British cookbook containing a curry recipe was Hannah Glasse's *Art of Cookery Made Plain and Easy* (1747). The recipe was essentially an aromatic stew flavoured with peppercorns and coriander seeds but in the 1796 edition, curry and cayenne (chilli) powder were added. Curry recipes are found in Dr William Kitchiner's *The Cook's Oracle* (1816), Mrs Dalgairn's *Practice of Cookery* (1829), Meg Dods's *The Cook and Housewife's Manual* (1826) and Maria Rundell's *Domestic Cookery*. First published in 1807, this work went through 65 editions by 1841. The editions edited by Emma Roberts, who had lived in India, contained many recipes for curries and other Indian dishes, some attributed to the King of Oudh.

Enterprising merchants began manufacturing commercial versions and promoted their health and gastronomical benefits. In 1784 Sorlie's Perfumery Warehouse advertised that curry 'renders the Stomac active in Digestion – the blood naturally free in Circulation – the mind vigorous – and contributes most of any food to an increase in the Human Race' (a hint at its alleged aphrodisiac powers). In 1844 Captain William White of the Bengal Army, manufacturer of Selim's Curry Paste (sold until the late 1930s), published a pamphlet: 'Curries: Their Properties and Healthful and Medicinal Qualities'. By the 1860s curry paste, mulligatawny paste and chutney were sold in large stores like Fortnum and Mason's, Halls of London and Crosse and Blackwell's shop in Soho Square. The most common ingredients in these powders were coriander seed, cumin seed, mustard seed, fenugreek, black pepper, chillies, turmeric and curry leaves and sometimes ginger, cinnamon, cloves and cardamom.

Imports of turmeric tripled between 1820 and 1841. The basic mixture is similar to that used today in southern India as well as the blends described by Colonel Kenney-Herbert and Dr Riddell.

Curry was fashionable among the elite, including the Prince Regent's set. But by the second half of the nineteenth century, curry had gained popularity among the urban middle classes, whose growing prosperity made them eager for new experiences. Indian fabrics, shawls, furnishings and food became fashionable. The memsahibs, who had once scorned Indian food at their own tables, now presented themselves as experts in Indian cuisine. Popular magazines printed recipes for curry and other Indian dishes. One reason for its popularity was economy: curry was an ideal way of using left-over meat and fish. In 1851 the anonymous author of *Modern Domestic Cookery* wrote: 'Curry, which was formerly a dish almost exclusively for the table of those who had made a long residence in India, is now so completely naturalized that few dinners are thought complete unless one is on the table.'[2]

Curry became so popular that in 1845 the Duke of Norfolk, at the height of the Irish famine, told a group of labourers that they should put a 'pinch of curry' into hot water to assuage their hunger, since in India 'a vast portion of the population use it; in fact, it is to them what potatoes are in Ireland'. This comment made the duke an object of considerable derision: *The Times* predicted 'the noble cuisinnier [*sic*] will go down to posterity with a pinch of curry powder in his hand', while the Yorkshire poet F. W. Moorman (1872–1919) referred to this speech in his poem *The Hungry Forties*:

> There was a papist duke that com aleng
> Wi' currypowders, an' he telled our boss

James Allen Sharwood introduced his line of Indian chutneys, pickles and curry powders in London in 1889.

> That when fowk's bellies felt pination's teng
> For bread, yon taink' powder they mun soss.[3]

The two most influential Victorian cookbooks, Eliza Acton's *Modern Cookery in all its Branches* (1845) and later editions of Isabella Beeton's *Household Management* (first published in 1861), devote entire chapters to curry. Unlike Colonel Kenney-Herbert's elaborate production, Mrs Beeton's curry takes only 50 minutes to prepare. The onions are sautéed with, not before, the meat, together with minced apple (which became a standard sweetening/souring agent in British and North American curries). The curry powder is added at the same time as the stock. Flour is used as a thickening agent, and coconut milk is replaced by cream. Mrs Beeton recommends the curry powder 'purchased at any respectable shop [as], generally, far superior and . . . more economical' than those made at home.

Cookbooks exclusively dedicated to Indian food appeared. Richard Terry, chef at the Oriental Club in London, published *Indian Cookery* in 1861. Daniel Santiagoe, an Indian cook and former domestic servant, wrote *The Curry Cook's Assistant: Curries and How to Make them in England in the Original Style* (1889, 3rd edn). In 1895 Henrietta Hervey, the wife of an Indian army officer (who brought her *dekchies*, or Indian pots, back with her from Bombay), published *A Curry Book: Anglo-Indian Cookery at Home*. Although she gives recipes for three curry powders – Madras, Bombay and Bengal – she is not opposed to the use of shop-bought mixtures.

Although Queen Victoria never visited India, she was fascinated by all things Indian. She collected Indian paintings and employed Indian servants dressed in exotic costumes, including two Indian cooks who prepared curry daily while she was at Osborne House. Her son Edward VII was a patron of the Savoy Hotel, which had a curry cook on the staff, and her grandson George V was said to have had little interest in any food except curry and Bombay duck.

Curry filtered down to the working classes where it enjoyed considerable popularity, because curry powders and curries were regarded as both economical and nutritious and because of its association with the Empire. Charles Elmé Francatelli, Queen Victoria's personal chef, included a curry recipe in his book *A Plain Cookery Book for the Working*

Classes (1861). In a poem by an anonymous author (actually Thackeray) that appeared in *Punch*'s *Poetical Cookery-Book*, the speaker, 'Samiwel', describes a domestic scene from working-class London:

> Three pounds of veal my darling girl prepares
> And chops it nicely into little squares
> Five onions next prepares the little minx
> The biggest are the best her Samiwel thinks
> And Epping butter, nearly half a pound
> And stews them in a pan until there brown'd
> What's next my dexterous little girl will do?
> She pops the meat into the savory stew
> With curry powder, tablespoonsfulls three
> And milk a pint (the richest that may be)
> And when the dish has stewed for half an hour
> A lemon's ready juice she'll o'er it pour
> Then, bless her, then she gives the luscious pot
> A very gentle boil – and serves quite hot
> P.S. Beef, mutton rabbit, if you wish
> Lobsters, or prawns, or any kind of fish
> Are fit to make A CURRY. 'Tis when done
> A dish for emperors to feed upon.[4]

The Twentieth Century

In the late nineteenth and early twentieth centuries, Britain was home to a few thousand Indians, mainly servants, students and ex-seamen from Bengal. Many came from the Sylhet region (now part of Bangladesh), which traditionally supplied cooks to the Portuguese and later the British. By 1920 there were a handful of Indian restaurants in London, including the Salut e Hind in Holborn, the Coronation Hotel and Restaurant, and cafés near the docks in the East End. One of the earliest restaurants to be called a curry house was the Shafi. Its employees were mainly ex-seamen, who later went on to start their own restaurants.

The first upmarket Indian restaurant was Veeraswamy's at 99 Regent Street in London, today one of the capital's finest Indian restaurants. It was opened in 1927 by Edward Palmer, a great-grandson of a Hyderabadi princess and an English

An early menu from Veeraswamy's, London's first upmarket Indian restaurant. It opened in 1927 and became a popular dining place for royalty and celebrities.

lieutenant general. He was also the founder of E. P. Veeraswamy & Co., Indian Food Specialists, which imported spices and curry pastes from India and sold them under the label Nizam's. Palmer had run the Indian restaurant at the British Empire Exhibition of 1924 at Wembley; it was so successful that he decided to make it permanent.[5]

Palmer's restaurant retained the Raj atmosphere of the exhibition café, with cane chairs, potted palms and Indian waiters wearing traditional bearers' uniforms. The menu listed vindaloos, Madras curries, dopiazas, coloured pilaus and other popular Anglo-Indian dishes; the less adventurous could dine on English rump steak and lamb cutlet. Famous clients included the Prince of Wales (later Edward VIII), King Gustav of Sweden, Charlie Chaplin and the King of Denmark. The restaurant was sold to the MP Charles Stewart and in 1997 purchased by Camellia and Namita Panjabi, who renovated it and restored its former cachet.

One of the by-products of Veeraswamy's was the publication of a delightful little cookbook, *Indian Cookery*, ostensibly by E. P. Veeraswamy himself, who tells his (fictional) life story in the preface. First published in London in 1936, the book has been reprinted dozens of times. His instructions distil the essence of Anglo-Indian curry-making:

- Onions should be thinly sliced and never be allowed to brown
- Curry powder or spices should be lightly fried for a few minutes to get rid of their raw flavour
- Ready made curry powder is perfectly acceptable since every ingredient in a genuine curry powder is identical to what is ground on the curry stone in Indian households.
- Those who speak of 'fresh ingredients' being used in

India know absolutely nothing beyond what their native Indian servant has told them.

- Any kind of fat can be used
- Milk or sour cream can substitute for coconut milk in many curries
- On no account thicken curry with flour. If the gravy is too thin, add coconut milk, milk or dried coconut and/ or evaporate with the lid off
- Apples and raisins are never used in Indian curries
- Curries should be served in separate dishes, never with rice as a border
- Curries should be eaten with a dessert spoon and fork
- Proper accompaniments include pappadums, chutneys, pickles, Bombay duck and sambals.[6]

After 1947 many immigrants found employment in the restaurant and catering businesses and opened hundreds of small restaurants of their own. Their customers were initially other South Asians as well as British men who had lived in India or were stationed there during the War. Their menus featured dishes found in the cookbooks and on the tables of the Raj.

Companies such as Noons, Pathaks (later Pataks) and S&A foods began to manufacture Indian spice mixtures and sauces, chutneys, pickles and other Indian products. In the 1960s the emergence of the counter-culture and the Beatles' visit to India contributed to the growing popularity of Indian food, as did Madhur Jaffrey's books and television cooking series in the 1970s.

The creation of Bangladesh in 1971 generated a new wave of immigrants who found employment in 'curry houses', the generic name for a generally downmarket Indian or Pakistani eating establishment. The curry house decor traditionally featured red flock wallpaper (perhaps an attempt to replicate the environment of Raj-era clubs). Most of the customers turned up just after 11 p.m., the closing time for pubs. 'Going out for a curry' after a night of hard drinking at weekends became a way of life for a certain segment of the population. Often the curries were prepared with ready-made sauces, giving the food a certain homogeneity. In his book, *The Curry Bible*, Pat Chapman lists the following sixteen curries as most popular in British Indian restaurants: balti, bhoona, dhansak, jalfrezi, keema, kofta, korma, madras, masala, medium, pasanda, patia, phall, roghan josh, tikka masala curry and vindaloo – a list not very different from those given in the *Indian Cookery Book* published in 1880.

How 'authentic' were their menus? The typical Indian restaurant menu throughout the world is largely an artificial creation. In Indian households, meals do not normally have a sequence of courses. The dishes arrive more or less at once and remain on the table throughout the meal. Most of the calories come from starch, either rice or bread, and dal (boiled lentils), supplemented by small amounts of meat, fish and vegetables, pickles, chutneys, salads and yogurt. The Western concept of a main course, usually meat, is alien to India, as are hors d'oeuvres and desserts.

To appeal to non-Indian customers, restaurant owners adapted Indian dishes to a Western format. As appetizers, they served street foods and snacks such as samosas, pakoras, kabobs and baskets of *papads* or *pappadum*, crunchy flat discs made from lentil flour and served with coriander and tamarind sauces. Dal was sometimes served as a soup, not as a core element of a meal. Sweets, normally eaten at festivals or as an afternoon snack, became desserts.

In the 1970s tandoori restaurants became popular (although the first tandoor, a clay oven, had been imported in

1959 by Veeraswamy's). All these establishments were essentially imitators of Moti Mahal restaurant opened in New Delhi in 1948 by Kundan Lal Gujral. A refugee from Pakistan, Kundan Lal invented tandoori chicken: pieces of chicken marinated in yogurt and spices and roasted in a tandoor, which he had built to order. To please richer palates (and, some claim, use left-over tandoori chicken), he created butter chicken – pieces of roasted chicken served in a tomato, cream and butter sauce – the precursor of chicken tikka masala. Nans and other breads and kabobs cooked on long skewers in the tandoor were featured on the menu. Moti Mahal was one

Balti dishes are prepared and served in wok-like pots called *karahis* or *karhais*.

of the very first restaurants in India serving Indian food that attracted a middle-class clientele.

The next sensation was balti cuisine, which started in south Birmingham in an area now called 'the balti triangle' and spread to other cities. Its origins are unclear. Some claim it originated in Baltistan, a province high in the Pakistan Himalayas, although the food there bears no resemblance to balti cuisine. Another explanation is that the word 'balti' means bucket in Hindi, perhaps a reference to the wok-like pot called a *karahi* or *karhai*. A similar dish is served in North America as *karahi gosht*, or frontier chicken (a reference to the North- West Frontier province).

To make a balti, pieces of marinated – usually precooked – meat, vegetables or seafood are stir-fried and served in a sauce of puréed onions, ginger, garlic, tomatoes, ground spices and fresh coriander. Aubergine, potato, mushrooms, corn, lentils and other ingredients may be added. A balti is cooked and served in the same pot and scooped up with pieces of baked bread. Side dishes and starters include fried onions, samosas, chutneys and pappadums. Often, patrons may bring their own alcoholic drinks. The popularity of the balti is easy to understand: it is delicious, easy to make, cheap and lets patrons create their own dishes and share them with others.

Balti and tandoori dishes were added to the menus of curry houses. The cooks adapted the 'hotness' of a dish to the diner's taste, and it became a sign of manliness to eat a very hot curry, washed down by prodigious amounts of beer. Vindaloos were hot, but the hottest of all, for reasons unknown, were called *phal*, which means 'fruit' in Hindi. These macho connotations led to the adoption of the song 'Vindaloo' as an unofficial anthem for English football fans during the 1998 World Cup.

Eating curry, the hotter the better, has become a feature of British pub and restaurant life.

In the 1960s and '70s curry recipes were popularized in cookbooks and magazines. Harvey Day's *Curries of India*, which contains recipes for all the familiar Anglo-Indian dishes, became a bestseller. Pat Chapman, founder of the Curry Club in 1982, has done the most to promote curry. His many books and publications give recipes for dishes found in UK curry houses and balti restaurants, making them accessible to non-Indians who want to make them at home.

To 'purists' who claim that the British public is being duped by restaurateurs serving inauthentic dishes, Chapman replies that commercial exigencies and the need for rapid service forces restaurants to adapt techniques and ingredients different from those used in home cooking, and that 'formula' restaurant-style curries can in any case be superb.

Since 1984 Cobra Beer has sponsored a guide to the hundred best curry restaurants and balti houses in Britain based on reports from Curry Club members.

In 1982 Camellia Panjabi opened Bombay Brasserie in Kensington with the aim of celebrating regional cooking and challenging the downmarket perception of Indian restaurants. Other top-end venues include the Red Fort, which opened in Soho in 1984 to serve upmarket northern Indian Muslim and tandoori dishes; the Panjabi sisters' Chutney Mary in Chelsea (1990), featuring dishes from six regions of India; Cyrus Todiwala's Café Spice Namaste (1991), which offers Goan, Parsee and other regional specialties; Zaikia; Chor Bazaar; and Cinnamon Club.

The latest episode in the saga of British curry is the emergence of very expensive Indian restaurants in London. In 2008 five Indian restaurants were awarded a Michelin star: Amaya, Benares, Quilon, Rasoi Vineet Bhatia and Tamarind. With their elegant decor, extensive wine lists, immaculate service and focus on regional ingredients, they are a far cry from the curry houses of old. Benares's Atul Kochhar (the first Indian chef to win a Michelin star) even represented London and the South-East in the BBC's *Great British Menu* competitions – the ultimate proof of how deeply Indian food has become integrated into British life.

3
The Colonies: The United States, Canada and Australia

Passage to India!
Cooling airs from Caucasus far, soothing cradle of man,
The river Euphrates flowing, the past lit up again.
Lo, soul, the retrospect, brought forward;
The old, most populous, wealthiest of Earth's lands,
The streams of the Indus and the Ganges, and their many affluent
(I, my shores of America walking to-day, behold, resuming all)

Walt Whitman, *Passage to India*, 1869

The United States

In the eighteenth century, immigrants from Britain brought with them to the United States the popular cookbooks of the day, including those of Hannah Glasse, Mrs Rundell and Mrs Beeton, which were soon published and sold in official and pirated editions. The first known curry recipe in North America was one for apple curry soup in the eighteenth-century manuscript of Catherine Moffatt Whipple (*b.* 1734), wife of a signatory of the Declaration of Independence.

A work considered by some to be the first truly American cookbook (as well as the first regional American cookbook) is Mary Randolph's *The Virginia Housewife, or Methodical Cook*

(1824). It contains a recipe for chicken curry 'after the East Indian manner', for catfish curry and for curry powder (equal amounts of turmeric, coriander seed, cumin seeds, white ginger, nutmeg, mace and cayenne pepper). Eliza Leslie's best-selling *Direction for Cookery in its Various Branches* (1840) contains recipes for 'Mulligatawany Soup as Made in India', chicken curry and chicken pulao. *The Housekeeper's Assistant* by Ann Allen (1845) contains recipes for curry, Malay curry and curry powder. Another influential figure in nineteenth-century American cookery was Catherine Beecher, author of *Domestic Receipt Book* (1846). Her generic recipe for curries starts with braising boiled chicken or veal in butter and some of the boiling water, and stewing it for twenty minutes with home-made curry powder, boiled rice, flour and the cooking liquids.

Before the American Revolution, wealthy American colonists ordered many luxuries from India via England and the Caribbean, among them tea, pepper, ginger, cardamom, saffron, turmeric, cumin and curry powder. Indian spices became more accessible to the middle classes after the East India Company lost its monopoly over trade with India in 1813. Boston's India Wharf opened in 1809 to accommodate ships going to and from India and China; in one day alone, nearly eighty ships from Calcutta unloaded their cargoes on its docks. Chicken curry, curried veal and lobster curry were standard items on the bills of fare of Boston taverns and eating houses in the 1820s and '30s.

While Americans were importing 'hot' spices from India, they were shipping large quantities of cold ice from New England's frozen ponds and rivers to Calcutta and Madras. 'Thus it appears', reflected Henry David Thoreau, who, like his fellow New England Transcendentalists, was enamoured with Indian philosophy, 'that the sweltering inhabitants of . . .

Madras and Bombay and Calcutta drink at my well', and that while he bathed 'in the stupendous and cosmogonal philosophy of the Bhagavad-Gita, the pure Walden water is mingled with the sacred water of the Ganges'. Whether Thoreau, a vegetarian, had the opportunity to try Indian food is not known. The number of Indians in America remained very small: a total of 716 arrivals between 1820 and 1900, most of them seamen and indentured servants.

Throughout the nineteenth century, curry recipes featured in popular cookbooks. *Miss Parloa's New Cookbook: A Guide to Marketing and Cooking* by the food editor at *Good Housekeeping* contains nine curry recipes, including mulligatawny soup, curry of cold meat and curried chicken in jelly. An article by the *New York Times* London correspondent on 25 November 1887, 'Curry for the Turkey' (a review of Daniel Santiagoe's *The Curry Cook's Assistant*), suggests that readers make a curry of their Thanksgiving left-overs instead of the usual hash.

One of the most popular curries in the southern United States was the Anglo-Indian dish country captain chicken, which many believed was invented in America. According to one explanation of its origin, a sea-captain who sailed into Charleston harbour with a shipload of spices from India was so graciously entertained by the city's hostesses that he repaid their hospitality by teaching their cooks to make a chicken curry, which was then named after him.

The earliest published recipe for country captain chicken appeared in Eliza Leslie's *New Cookery Book* (1857). In the early twentieth century Alexander Filippino, the chef at the fashionable New York restaurant Delmonico's, made his own version that included currants and slivered almonds.

President Franklin D. Roosevelt became a fan of country captain chicken after tasting it in Warm Springs, Georgia, where he eventually built a home. One of his visitors, General George S. Patton, also loved the dish, which in 2000 the Pentagon made into one of its packaged MREs (Meals Ready to Eat) given to soldiers in the field.

The dish made such an impression on the prominent food teacher and writer James Beard that he taught it at his cooking school in New York. Later it found an impassioned champion in the New York food writer Cecily Brownstone, who has been called a 'one woman preservation society' for the dish. For nearly four decades she exposed myths about country captain chicken and rooted out impostors. 'Using a breast, can you imagine?' she said in a telephone interview in 1991. 'I don't want to give names – but can you imagine that someone actually used cream? Cream! And they called it country captain! It is very discouraging.'[1] She too preferred Filippino's recipe, published it many times and insisted on getting it included 'for the record' in dozens of cookbooks, including the classic *The Joy of Cooking*.

Another very popular American dish that may have originated in the south was curried chicken salad – pieces of cooked chicken, celery and sometimes pieces of pineapple or apple served in a mayonnaise dressing flavoured with curry powder. Oysters were inexpensive and abundant in the nineteenth century – in 1874 there were more than 850 oyster bars in New York City alone – and curries were a favourite method of serving them both in the US and Britain.

The first Indian chef in North America – and one of the earliest celebrity 'bad boy' chefs – was Ranji Smile. He was discovered by the New York restaurateur Richard Sherry at London's Savoy Hotel and brought to New York in 1899 to prepare curries at Sherry's eponymous new restaurant on Fifth Avenue. Dubbed 'King of the Curry Chefs' by reporters, Smile became an overnight success by 'initiating the fashionable set in New York into the mysteries and delights of East Indian cooking', according to a *Harper's Bazaar* article called 'A Chef From India: Women Go Wild Over Him'. 'The fancy for curries, which is the foundation for all India dishes, seems to have take possession of every one who has eaten of them', reported the *Los Angeles Times*.

Smile (his name was probably an invention) claimed to have learned his craft in his native Karachi and in Calcutta and Bombay hotels. He told reporters that Americans cannot make good curries because they are in too much of a hurry and use the same mixture for beef, chicken and fish. Curries must be simmered slowly, never boiled and are not invariably hot.

Sadly, publicity went to Ranji Smile's head. He started calling himself 'Prince' and claimed to be the fourth son of the Emir of Baluchistan, a graduate of Cambridge University and a personal friend of King Edward VII. Smile left Sherry's to open his own restaurants, which failed. He was arrested for drunkenness, disorderly conduct and violating federal labour laws by bringing in illegal workers from India. Smile was reduced to giving culinary demonstrations and married a succession of ever-younger American women.

Success went to the head of Ranji Smile, who came to New York as a curry chef in 1899, and began calling himself a prince and friend of royalty.

In 1913 Ranji Smile left for Delhi with his newest wife to open 'a real Indian restaurant for the poor American tourists, who never have had anything good to eat since they began to look up Kipling's country'. There is no record that such an establishment ever saw the light of day or that Ranji Smile left behind any culinary legacy in his adopted land.

By the end of the 1920s New York had half a dozen Indian restaurants known for their fiery curries, among them The Rajah on 44th Street, west of Broadway, and Ceylon India Inn on 49th Street, which operated until the mid-1960s. Thanks to racial exclusion laws, the country's Indian population remained very small: only around 3,000 people in 1930, many of them students living in New York City.

American food writers were fascinated with Indian food but, because their contacts with India and Indians were limited, they often substituted fantasy for reality. The author of a 1941 article in the *New York Times* rapturously describes a visit to an unnamed Indian restaurant where the 'almond-eyed Hindu chef in his wondrously wound snowy turban' smiles enigmatically. She could almost hear the muted music of *The Song of India* as she peered into the 'steaming caldrons of strange, spicy mélanges . . . with their pungent perfumes' filled with that 'rare Oriental ragout that is called a curry'. Curry sauce is described as a marvellous medley – 'incredibly involved for the average occidental' – made from tomato paste, green peppers, and between twenty and forty spices. The unnamed restaurant's eclectic offerings include pink curries from Java and Ceylon, Hawaiian chicken curry, dark spicy lamb curry, and a mixed vegetable curry with baked bananas, cashew nuts, papaya cubes and okra – 'the true foods of occult India'.[2]

In 1952 the prominent food writer and editor Florence Brobeck published *Cooking with Curry* (New York, 1951), the first American book devoted entirely to curry. As she explains in her introduction, most cookbooks on the subject 'frighten the wits out of a plain American cook' because they call for a multitude of pots, sieves, colanders, a mortar to grind exotic spices, strange fruits 'only available if you happen to know a sailor who's due from the South Seas', as well as a knowledge of various Indian dialects to translate Hindu weights and measures and the native words for spices. She provides menus for middle-class households that feature Hawaiian, Algerian, Australian, New Zealand, Cantonese, Chinese, Japanese, Cajun, West Indian and Turkish curries as well several quasi-Indian dishes with names like Bombay, Calcutta or Bengalese curries. With a few exceptions, all call for the use of ready-made curry powder.

After World War Two, Bengali seamen who had jumped ship and settled in Harlem opened halal butcher shops and small Indian eating establishments on New York's Upper West Side. Some of these men married Puerto Rican and African-American women. Another hybrid community arose in California's Sacramento Valley where Punjabi men, mainly Sikhs, had emigrated as farmers in the early twentieth century. After racial exclusion laws in 1917 ended immigration by 'non-whites', many married local Mexican women. Their community, which came to total 400 couples, became known as 'Mexican Hindus'. Their cuisine combined elements of Mexican and Punjabi food. Chicken curry, roti and something called 'Hindu pizza' still feature on the menu of Rasul's El Ranchero Mexican restaurant in Yuba City, California.

The 1964 World's Fair in New York raised the profile of Indian food in America. The dining room in the Indian Pavilion received enthusiastic reviews from Craig Claiborne for its elegant design, the 'intoxicating politesse' of the staff and the excellence of the food, 'admirably spiced but without

Antonia Alvarez and Rullia Singh, photographed in 1917, were part of California's 'Hindu-Mexican' community composed of Indian men who married local Mexican women.

the overpowering hotness that is frequently and often mistakenly ascribed to Indian cuisine'.[3] But Claiborne, who often reviewed Indian restaurants for the *New York Times*, complained that it was difficult to find an Indian restaurant of unfailing distinction in Manhattan. However, he did have high praise for Gaylord's Restaurant, whose chef came from the original Moti Mahal, especially its tandoori chicken. He noted that the menu featured several dishes of the 'curry' type – the quote marks indicating that, in his view, this was not a legitimate name for an Indian dish.

In 1974 Madhur Jaffrey published *An Invitation to Indian Cookery*, which Craig Claiborne called 'perhaps the best Indian cookbook in English'. In the introduction, she states:

> To me the word 'curry' is as degrading to India's great cuisine as the term 'chop suey' was to China's . . . 'Curry' is just a vague, inaccurate word which the world has picked up from the British, who, in turn, got it mistakenly from us . . . If 'curry' is an oversimplified name for an ancient cuisine, then 'curry powder' attempts to oversimplify (and destroy) the cuisine itself.[4]

In her best-selling *A Taste of India* (1985), Madhur Jaffrey uses the term 'curry' for only one dish. In 1980 Julie Sahni published her best-selling *Indian Classical Cookery*. She writes that in north Indian cooking there is no real equivalent to Western or British curry powder or, for that matter, any dish known as a curry, the closest thing being a *salan* – a meat dish with a thin gravy (a term rarely found in British recipe books). However, this strict usage seems to be a thing of the past: Madhur Jaffrey called a later work *The Ultimate Curry Bible*, which contains information and recipes for curries from around the world. Raghavan Iyer extends the definition even further in his book *660 Curries* (New York, 2008): the 660 recipes include salads, dals, kabobs, breads and beverages.

With the end of restrictive immigration laws in 1965, hundreds of thousands of Indian professionals emigrated to the US, part of the famous 'brain drain'. By 2005, 2.4 million people of South Asian origin lived in the United States. However, unlike in Britain, only a small minority are of Bangladeshi origin.

By the 1970s there were Indian shopping/restaurant districts in all US cities, including Jackson Heights in Queens, New York; Chicago's Devon Avenue; Pioneer Boulevard in Los Angeles; and Hillcroft Avenue in Houston. Today virtually every suburb and town has Indian grocery stores that stock spices, pickles, fruits and vegetables, and frozen and packaged meals and breads. Indian products can also be found on the shelves of most supermarket chains.

Of US cities, New York has the largest number of Indian restaurants as well as the widest range of levels and cuisines, ranging from 'dhabas' – tiny hole-in-the-wall establishments

New York, Chicago, Toronto and other North American cities have Indian shopping and restaurant districts, like this one on First Avenue between 5th and 6th Streets, Manhattan.

that serve kabobs, biryanis and other north Indian dishes to taxi drivers – to elegant upmarket establishments like Tabla and the Michelin-starred Devi, which opened in 2004.

In general, Americans are less familiar with Indian food than the British. One reason is the lack of close historical ties between the US and India; another is the prevalence of Chinese, Mexican and Thai restaurants, which satisfy Americans' growing taste for spicy foods. There are no equivalents of British curry houses with their flock wallpapers and standardized menus, and no balti restaurants. Most Indian restaurants in the US serve a hodgepodge of Punjabi, north Indian Muslim and southern Indian dishes. A survey of the restaurant menus posted on the website menupages.com indicates that the term 'curry' appears much less frequently than it does in the UK, and in many cases is not used at all.

Canada[5]

In the eighteenth and nineteenth centuries, most immigrants to Upper Canada (now the province of Ontario) came from the British Isles and brought with them the popular cookbooks of the day. The first Canadian cookbooks, such as *Mrs Nourse's Modern Practical Cookery* (1845) and *Mrs Clarke's Cookery Book* (1883), contain recipes for curried oysters, tripe, chicken, rabbit, lobster and potatoes. Mrs Clarke observes that while old Anglo-Indians know how to make a good curry, it is rarely found in North America except in the house of someone who has spent many years in India. (She adds that even in India, the art of curry-making is declining.)

Spices played an important role in enlivening the pickled, dried and salted meats and fish that were the early settlers' daily fare during the long winters. In the 1830s a pioneer woman wrote in her diary: 'We consume more in the way of ketchups, sauces, curry powder, etc. than we used to do at home on account of the many months we are without fresh meat.' An unnamed moose hunter wrote in *Gentleman's Magazine* in 1872: 'I never went out without one or more small cases of curry powder that I brought with me from home.'

Top civil servants who rotated between posts in England and the colonies introduced curry to upper-class circles. In 1877 Governor General Lord Dufferin, formerly British Under-Secretary for India, served a curry to his guests at a camping expedition on the Winnipeg River. Curries and Anglo-Indian dishes such as mulligatawny soup were common at official banquets in Upper Canada (although not, of course, in Lower Canada, modern Quebec, where French culinary tradition prevailed).

Like those of the US and Australia, Canada's immigration policy excluded non-whites. In 1962 the most blatantly racist provisions were overturned; in 1976 a new policy based admission on education, employment skills, language abilities and family sponsorship. The 2001 Canadian census reported that over 900,000 residents of Canada were of Indian origin – 3.1 per cent of the entire population – including a sizeable number from Trinidad and Tobago and Guyana.

Most immigrants settled in Toronto and Vancouver, where there are thriving and diverse Indian food cultures. Samosas and Caribbean curry-flavoured patties are sold everywhere and have almost become national dishes. The restaurant culture is thriving: Toronto has North America's only Chettinad restaurant, as well as establishments serving Keralan, East African Ismaili, Guyanese, Trinidadian and Sri Lankan food. Vancouver is the site of one of Canada's top restaurants, Vij, an upmarket establishment on a par with the Michelin-starred London restaurants.

Australia

Early immigrants to Australia came almost exclusively from the British Isles, and in the nineteenth century all the popular British cookbooks of the day were sold in Australian bookshops. The relatively few cookbooks written by Australians – *The Australian Cook* (1876) by Alfred Wilkinson, Mrs Lance Rawson's *Cookery Book and Household Hints* (1878), *Australian Plain Cookery* (3rd edn, 1884) and *Mrs Maclurcan's Cookery Book: A Collection of Practical Recipes Specially Suitable for Australia* (1898) – followed the English model and all contained curry recipes. For example, a suggested menu in Mrs Maclurcan's book, written for middle-class families, features curried mutton and rice, cabbage and potatoes, cheese canapés and baked apples in butter.

That curry was well known in nineteenth-century Australia is obvious from a tongue-in-cheek article by the Australian novelist Marcus Clarke, who despised the nouveau riches' worship of all things French and urged that curry be made the national dish:

> The basis of our regenerated Australian food system must be the curry – a curry of kid, mixed with three eggs, the white of a coconut scraped to a powder, two chillies, and half a dozen slices of pineapple . . . The small river crayfish are excellent material, while he who has never eaten a young wombat treated with coriander seeds, turmeric, green mango and dry ginger has not used his opportunities. When I become rich enough to benefit my fellow creatures, I shall take a shop in Collinstreet [in Melbourne] . . . and building a bamboo veranda, will establish a Curry House. Nothing but curry and pale ale will be dispensed and my waiters will be

> Chinname [*sic*], the best servants in the world dressed in spotless white robes.[6]

Starting in the 1830s, small groups of Afghans (a term that also included people from the Middle East and India) came with their camels to work in the outback, where only camels could survive the harsh climate and terrain. Today their only legacy is the wild camels that wander about the outback, and the name of the Ghan Railway that runs between Adelaide and Darwin. Between 1901 and 1947 a White Australia policy prohibited and deported non-white immigrants. Indian

The Australian novelist Marcus Clarke (1846–1881) so disliked his countrymen's adulation of French food that he suggested curry be made the national dish.

Keen's Curry Powder was developed in Tasmania by Joseph Keen in the early 1860s and remains a popular curry flavouring in Australia.

independence in 1947 and independence and civil war in Sri Lanka resulted in a large influx of Anglo-Indians (descendants of British fathers and Indian mothers) and Sri Lankan burghers (Sri Lankans of mixed Dutch, Portuguese, European and Sinhalese/Tamil descent).

The White Australia policy was abolished in 1978. By 2006 nearly half of all Australians were either born overseas or had at least one parent who was born abroad. Many of the immigrants came from India, Fiji and South-East Asia. This influx coincided with the Australian culinary revolution that attended the explosion of the wine industry, and today Australia has one of the world's most diverse food cultures. Chinese, Thai, Indonesian, Vietnamese and Indian restaurants are ubiquitous in Australian towns and cities. As one blogger writes:

> These days, just about every Australian can walk into a restaurant and order a *nasi goreng* or a *buoi phuc trach* or a bowl of shito sauce . . . [and] just about every Australian

can cook a fancy-schmancy exotic meal at home . . . Gone are the days of roast dinners and veal forcemeat and the great Australian curry made out of chump steak, sultanas, banana, strawberry jam, and a teeny pinch of Keen's curry powder for that proper spicy Indian flavour.[7]

4
The Indian Diaspora: The Caribbean, Mauritius, Sri Lanka and Fiji

She pack up all her curry and she runaway
Leaving me to worry myself sick each day,
I went and rome, from dust to dawn
Come back home to find the curry gone.
Mighty Trini, *Curry Tabanca*

While the British brought curry to their English-speaking colonies, it was Indians themselves who took their eating habits to the rest of the empire. In the nineteenth century, the vast subcontinent, ravaged by disease, famine and poverty, was fertile territory for recruiting soldiers for British armies and agricultural workers for the empire's sugar, palm oil, coffee and tea plantations.

The abolition of the slave trade in the British Empire in 1807 and of slavery itself in 1833 created a labour shortage in Fiji, Mauritius, Trinidad and Tobago, Guyana, Malaysia and South Africa, since former slaves no longer wanted to perform back-breaking plantation work. So the British government set up offices in Calcutta and Madras to recruit Indians as indentured labourers to work for a certain period of time, typically five or ten years. They received basic provisions and a minimal salary, followed by either a free passage home or free land. All but a handful chose the latter option.

Between 1834, when the first group of indentured labourers arrived in Mauritius, and 1917, when the system was abolished, nearly 1.5 million Indians emigrated to other parts of the British Empire. In the western hemisphere, 240,000 Indians went to British Guiana (now Guyana), 144,000 to Trinidad and 36,000 to Jamaica. Around 150,000 labourers migrated to South Africa. Others went to Fiji and Malaysia. Most of the immigrants came from either north and central India – the present-day states of Bihar, Orissa and Uttar Pradesh – or Tamil Nadu and Andhra Pradesh in the south.

The British authorities also made arrangements with the French and Dutch to send indentured workers to their colonies. Between 1853 and 1885, eighty thousand Indians migrated to Martinique, Guadeloupe and French Guyana. A smaller group went to Dutch Guyana, now Surinam, where they became known as Hindoestanen. When Surinam gained its independence in 1975, many migrated to the Netherlands.

Trinidad and Tobago

Over 40 per cent of the one million inhabitants of Trinidad and Tobago are of Indian origin; another 40 per cent are Afro-Trinidadian; while the remaining 20 per cent are of Chinese, European and Middle Eastern descent. Although Trinidadian cuisine combines elements of all these backgrounds, curry and other Indian dishes have become symbols of national identity and feature in popular Calypso and Soca songs.

Most Indo-Trinidadians came from north-east and central India and spoke a language called Bhojpuri. These origins explain certain features of Indo-Trinidadian food. For example, whole wheat flour is never used in Trinidadian breads (rotis) as it is in India, because wheat was not grown in the immigrants' home regions and the first flour they encountered would have been imported white flour. A pinch of baking powder is always added to these breads. Phulorie, sahenna, kurma and other fried savoury snacks are similar to those found in the immigrants' ancestral regions. The basic ingredients of a typical Trinidadian spice mixture – cumin, coriander, fenugreek and turmeric – are what would be used in a peasant household here.

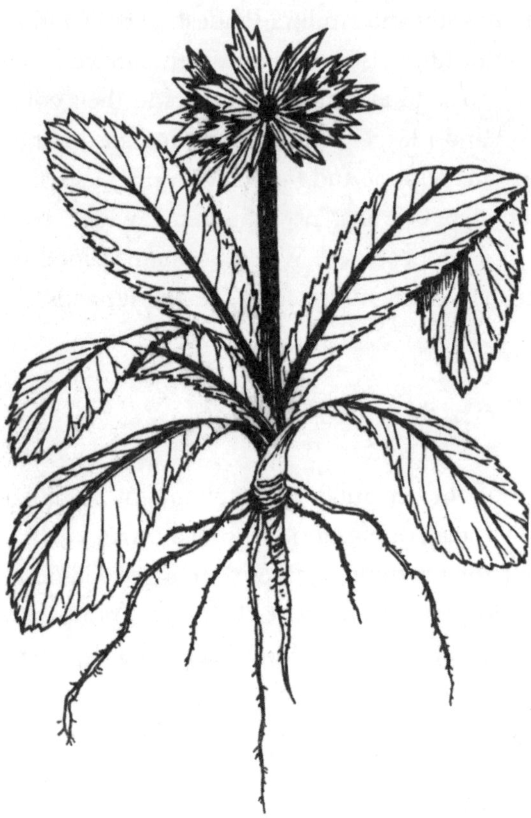

Bandhaniya or shadow beni is a local herb used as a substitute for coriander in Trinidadian cuisine.

Callaloo refers both to the leaf of the dasheen plant (a form of taro) and to a popular Jamaican and Trinidadian stew.

On their arrival, immigrants received daily rations of rice, dal, coconut oil or ghee, sugar and salt, turmeric and sometimes salted or dried fish and onions. Substitution was essential, since ingredients such as curry leaves, fresh coriander and mint were not grown locally. The substitute for coriander is a local herb called shado(w) beni that grows wild in drainage ditches. The chilli pepper used in Trinidadian curries is the very fiery scotch bonnet, so-called because it looks like a little pleated bonnet. In place of the spinach-like greens called 'sag' in India, Trinidadians and Jamaicans use callaloo, the leaf of the dasheen plant (a form of taro). Callaloo is also the name of a soup cooked with coconut milk, crab, okra, chillies and herbs.

In a typical Trinidadian curry the meat (usually chicken or goat) or fish is first marinated in garlic, onion, chillies, shadow beni and 'seasonings' – a tied bundle of chopped chive, parsley, shadow beni and garlic purchased in the

A roadside stand in Trinidad advertises its daily specials.

market. The cook browns the onions and garlic in oil, sautés a paste of curry powder mixed with a little water (a distinctive Caribbean technique) and adds the meat and marinade. At the end a little roasted cumin powder, a typical Trinidadian spice, is sprinkled to impart aroma. Sometimes a little local rum is added.

A characteristic feature of Trinidadian curries is the use of a ready-made curry powder, which gives them a certain consistency of flavour. The best-known manufacturers are Turban Brands, founded by a Sikh in 1956, and Chief, which is somewhat 'hotter'. However, 'authentic' Indian food also has a certain cachet and home cooks grind their own spice mixtures on special occasions.

Curries are accompanied by chutneys and sauces, including mango kuchela, a mango and mustard oil pickle, and 'mother-in-law', a fiery vegetable relish. Rotis are used both to scoop up the curry and as a wrapper to hold a filling.

In Trinidad, the word 'roti' also refers to a popular street food that has been known as the country's national dish. A large thick roti coated with ground yellow peas is wrapped around a meat, fish or vegetable curry, enclosed in wax paper or foil and eaten on the move. Another popular street food is 'doubles', a sandwich composed of two pieces of turmeric-flavoured fried roti filled with curried chickpeas and topped with spicy chutneys and chilli sauce. It is very similar to the Indian snack *chole bhature*.

Other distinctive Trinidadian breads are 'buss-up-shut' roti (named after a 'bursted-up shirt'), a flaky roti torn into ragged pieces; dal puri roti, fried bread stuffed with spiced lentils; sada roti, a plain white bread often made at home; and oil roti, a flaky paratha.

Guyana

In Guyana (formerly British Guyana), a small country in the north-east corner of South America, 43 per cent of the population are of Indian origin. The cuisine is similar to that of Trinidad and Tobago. Curries, a common main course, are usually served with rotis made from white flour and accompanied by relishes and pickles. The standard cooking liquid is coconut milk. Hotness comes from wiri wiri, a small local fragrant and fiery locally grown chilli. Although Guyanese curries are generally fiercely hot, some people also eat spicy pickles as a condiment or even take a bite out of a fresh chilli with each mouthful. Tartness comes from tomato, tamarind or green mango.

Fish curries are very popular in Guyana, especially when made from the freshwater fish that live in irrigation canals and rivers. Vegetables are often added to curries; popular combinations include chicken and squash, duck and potato, mutton and aubergine, shrimp and pumpkin, green beans and dried fish, and crab and aubergine. Vegetables that were originally grown in temperate climates, such as cauliflower, peas and carrots, did not become part of the culinary tradition as they did in India.

Jamaica

Although people of Indian origin constitute only 3 per cent of Jamaica's population, traditional Indian foods such as 'curry goat', roti and callaloo are now seen as 'Jamaican'. (Jamaicans sometimes name their food for the cooking technique: curry goat, stew chicken, jerk pork, steam fish and so on.) The national dish is saltfish (salted cod) and ackee (a tropical fruit) made with black pepper and scotch bonnet peppers. Curry goat, served on festive occasions, is cooked with prepared curry powder and scotch bonnet chillies in coconut milk and often served with rice and peas (kidney beans or pigeon peas). A soup called 'mannish water' containing a goat's head and other parts (including the penis), tomatoes, vegetables and chillies is believed to have aphrodisiac powers and is traditionally served to grooms on their wedding night.

A local twist is given to the classic British oxtail stew by the addition of beans, allspice (known locally as pimento) and scotch bonnet peppers. Beef patties, spiced ground meat in a dough pocket similar to an empanada, are popular snacks not only in Jamaica but also in Toronto and other North American cities with a large Caribbean population.

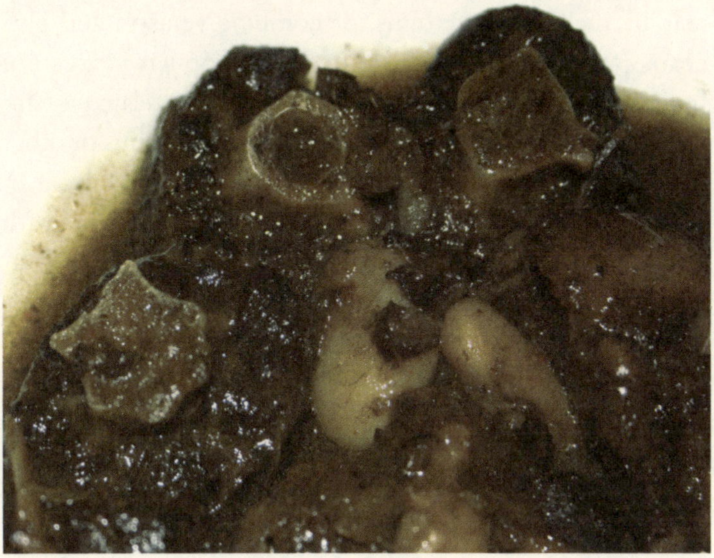

A spicy oxtail stew made with beans is a Jamaican version of a classic British dish.

Mauritius

An island nation in the Indian Ocean 500 miles east of Madagascar and 3,000 miles from India, Mauritius is a linguistic and culinary melting pot. Two-thirds of the population are of Indian origin (52 per cent Hindus, 13 per cent Muslims), 30 per cent are Franco-Mauritian or creoles and 3 per cent Chinese. Although the official language is English, most people speak a French-based Creole. Mauritius was colonized by the Dutch from 1598 to 1715, by the French from 1715 to 1815 and by the British from 1815 to 1968. Starting in the 1830s, the British brought in nearly half a million indentured labourers, mainly from north-eastern India, to work on the sugar plantations.

Mauritian cuisine is an intriguing mixture of African, Dutch, French and Indian ingredients and techniques. A curry may be made with octopus, or combine venison and lilva beans (a slightly sweet and bitter bean popular in western India), or chicken and prawns. *Vindaille* (a word related to vindaloo) is prepared by marinating fresh tuna, octopus or other seafood in mustard, saffron, chillies, garlic, oil and vinegar. A popular Indian-Mauritian snack is *dalpuri* – bread filled with curried lentils, *rougaille* (a spicy tomato-based sauce), chutneys and vegetable pickle.

Those who like to speculate about what Indian cuisine would have been like had the French conquered India instead of the British need only look at the sophisticated cuisine of Mauritius. An excellent collection of hundreds of recipes can be found at www.ile-maurice.tripod.com.

Sri Lanka

Sri Lanka, a small island in the Indian Ocean (until 1972 called Ceylon), is home to a society with a rich colonial past and a cuisine that is a mosaic of Sinhalese, Tamil, Indian, Dutch, Portuguese, Malay and British influences.

As a producer of spices and a stopover for ships plying the spice routes, in ancient times Sri Lanka was visited by merchants from the Middle East, Persia and South-east Asia. The Portuguese arrived in 1505 but were expelled by the Dutch in 1653; they in turn lost the island to the British in 1792. Ten years later, Ceylon became a British crown colony. In the nineteenth century, the British established tea, cinnamon, rubber, sugar, coffee and indigo plantations on the island and brought in thousands of indentured labourers from Tamil Nadu to work on them.

More than 80 per cent of Sri Lanka's population are Sinhalese, their ancestors having come from northern India thousands of years ago; they are mainly Buddhists. Around 10 per cent are Hindu Tamils. Sri Lanka also has small minorities of Muslims, who can trace their lineage to Arabs and Indians; Malays, brought by the Dutch; and Burghers – people of mixed European (especially Dutch) and Sinhalese or Tamil descent. In recent decades, many Burghers have emigrated to Australia, Canada and Britain, taking their eating habits with them.

The classic Sri Lanka cookbook, *The Ceylon Daily News Cookery Book* (first published in 1929 and still used today) by Hilda Deutrom, herself a Burgher, illustrates this diversity. It has separate chapters on British and Anglo-Indian dishes (for example, mulligatawny soup and kedgeree); rice and curries; sambals; chutneys and pickles; Sinhalese recipes; Tamil recipes; Sinhalese and Tamil sweets; Dutch and Portuguese sweets; and 'short eats' – a vivid local term for hors d'oeuvres and afternoon snacks.

Rice is the staple served with curries, boiled or made into two distinctive local products: hoppers, disc-shaped sautéed breads made of fermented rice flour and coconut milk, and string hoppers, steamed thin vermicelli. Both Tamil and Singhalese cuisines make extensive use of tamarind, Maldive fish (dried fermented bonito), coconut milk and fresh coconut. In Anglo-Indian recipe books, a Ceylon curry usually meant a seafood or fish curry with a coconut gravy.

A typical Sri Lankan curry powder is similar to the ones used in southern India and contains coriander, fennel, cumin, fenugreek, curry leaves, dried coconut, mustard seeds and chillies. Aromatic spices such as cinnamon and cardamom are added to Muslim meat-based dishes. Singhalese curries are classified by colour: white curries are milder with a more subtle flavour; black curries are made with spices roasted to create a deep, rich flavour; and red curries are made with plenty of

A Sri Lankan meal features such dishes as fish curry, green beans, mango pickle, egg and string hoppers (rice noodles).

red chillies. Like some South-east Asian curries, they often include lemon grass and pandanus (screwpine) leaves.

One of the most famous Sri Lankan Burgher culinary creations is *lamprais* (also spelled *lampries* and pronounced 'lampreese'), a kind of mini-rijsttafel. Its components are small mounds of ghee rice (rice sautéed in ghee and aromatic spices before boiling), an elaborate curry made from four meats, an ash gourd or banana curry, *balanchan*, chilli and onion sambal, and *frikkadels* (spicy meatballs of Dutch origin). All these items are wrapped in a steamed or roasted banana leaf to make a parcel that is held together by *ekels* – ribs of a coconut palm leaf. The parcels are warmed in the oven and brought to the table on a platter. Each guest receives at least one and unwraps it, savouring the aroma of spices and the fragrance of the banana leaf. The correct composition of a *lamprais* is the subject of heated dispute among Sri Lankans, especially those living abroad who have fond memories of the dish from their childhood.

Fiji

Nearly half of the population of Fiji, an island nation in the south Pacific, are descendants of 60,000 Indians brought by the British in the late 1890s to work on the sugar plantations. Fijian cuisine is a melange of Melanesian, Polynesian, Indian, Chinese and Western elements. Fijian curries are made with breadfruit, yam, cassava, taro root and leaves, and seafood, and usually contain coconut milk. Flavourings include garlic, ginger, turmeric, coriander, fenugreek, cumin, soy sauce and chillies. An unusual home-style curry is 'tinned fish' curry, made with canned tuna, mackerel or salmon. From Fiji, curries and curry powder spread to Tonga, Samoa and other islands in the Pacific, where they are often served with boiled taro or breadfruit as the starch.

5
Africa

She was nothing special, she wasn't merry
She wasn't even very pretty
But I see her in front of her stove
And I smell her delicious bobotie.

The cooking pots taught me
Bobotie is quite a job
If you don't know the art
And without my wife
I'll never manage the recipe.
Ddisselblom, 'Bobotie'

Africa has been a meeting ground for many civilizations. Arab traders visited the east coast as early as the second century AD. The Portuguese began exploring the coast of Africa in 1419 in search of a sea route to the source of the lucrative spice trade; in 1488 Bartolomeu Dias rounded the Cape of Good Hope. The Portuguese retained their colonies in Angola and Mozambique until the 1970s. Meanwhile, the Dutch and the British developed a strong presence, especially in southern and eastern Africa.

South Africa

South African food is often described as a 'rainbow' cuisine that mirrors the country's diverse ethnicities: Dutch (later called Afrikaaner), British, French, Malaysian, Indian and African.

In 1651 the Dutch East India Company established a settlement at the Cape of Good Hope to provide food and supplies for ships sailing between the Netherlands and the Dutch East Indies – a seventeenth-century truck stop. The colonists, who came from Dutch, French Huguenot and German stock, established permanent settlements and brought in slaves from Indonesia and India to work on their farms and in their kitchens.[1] They and their descendants became known as Cape Malays (Malay was the lingua franca of trade). Today, an estimated 180,000 Cape Malays live in South Africa, mainly in Cape Town.

In 1806 the British took control of the Cape and the colonists moved north in the Great Trek to settle in what became the provinces of Orange Free State, Transvaal and KwaZulu Natal. The British brought in 150,000 indentured labourers to work on their sugar, banana, tea and coffee plantations. Most were from southern India; a smaller group came from Bihar, Orissa and Uttar Pradesh. From the 1880s onwards they were joined by Indian businessmen, traders and lawyers (including a young Mahatma Gandhi). Many of these 'passenger Indians' came from Gujarat on India's west coast. They opened small restaurants and shops to sell spices and Indian condiments.

Celebrated for their cooking skills, the Cape Malays were much in demand as cooks in the early Dutch settlers' homes. Trade links with Indonesia ensured a supply of aromatic spices that were used with a free hand in stews, curries (called kerries), sausages and baked goods. By the middle of the eighteenth century, the dominant cooking style bore little resemblance to that of Holland and 'owe[d] as much to the East as to the West'.[2]

Several Cape Malay dishes became such a part of the South African way of life that the South African writer Laurens van der Post called them 'almost sacramental substances'.[3] Bobotie is a dish of finely minced beef or lamb, flavoured with curry powder (the original version was made with fresh spices), onions, garlic and lemon leaves, topped with a savoury custard and baked in the oven. It often includes almonds, raisins and apricots. There are many variations, including some made with fish. A classic recipe is found in Hildagonda Duckitt's (1840–1905) pioneering collection *Hilda's 'Where is it?' of Recipes*, which was first published in 1891 and went through many editions. Her book also includes recipes for chicken

One of the classic dishes of South African Cape Malay cuisine, bobotie.

Another popular South African Cape Malay dish, *sosatie*.

curry, a cucumber curry (made with minced mutton, bread and curry powder) and *sosatie*. From the Malay words for skewered meat and spiced sauce, *sosatie* is a mutton kabob marinated in onions, curry powder, chillies, garlic and tamarind water and roasted on skewers over an open fire.

Another classic South African/Cape Malay dish is *bredie*, a tomato and lamb stew made by sautéing onions, meat and vegetables, adding chillies and spices such as ginger, coriander, cinnamon and cloves, and then simmering in a cast-iron pot to create a thick curry-like stew. An edible water lily called *waterblommetjie* is often added. Another hybrid is a *koeksister*, a deep-fried fritter served in a sugar syrup flavoured with ginger, cardamom and cinnamon – a combination of an Indian *gulab jamun* and a European pastry.

Curries, or *kerries*, are enjoyed by all sections of the population in South Africa, including Zulus, the largest ethnic group. They are flavoured with both freshly ground fresh spices and Malay-style curry powder, which is generally milder

The most famous Indo-South African dish is bunny chow, a meat curry served in a hollowed-out loaf of Western-style bread.

than Indian-style curries; fruit is a common ingredient. Hilda Gerber's *Traditional Cookery of the Cape Malays* (1957) includes recipes for *giema* (keema or minced meat) *kerrie*; *groema kerri* seasoned with a special curry powder (not described) sold in Indian shops; *bahia kerri* flavoured with star fennel; and *pinang kerri* flavoured with lemon leaves. *Kerries* are served with *atjars*, Indian-style vegetable pickles; *blatjang*, a chutney-like condiment of Indonesian-Malay origin made with apricots, quinces and raisins; sliced bananas; chutneys; sambals, side dishes of grated fruit or vegetables with chillies; and rice.

In her compilation *Indian Delights* (published in the early 1960s), Zuleikha Mayat wrote that most of the Indian immigrants to South Africa came from poor rural backgrounds, which was reflected in their cookery. Lentils, beans, rice, flour rotis and mealie rice (crushed corn kernels boiled to look like rice) were dietary mainstays. The Hindu Gujaratis, who arrived as 'passenger Indians', were generally more affluent and enjoyed a more upmarket cuisine; the Muslim Gujaratis elaborated the preparation of meat dishes, 'making subtle distinctions between different grouping of condiments and producing sensitively different aromas and eating experiences'. The recipes in the chapter called 'Curries' mirror these diverse traditions.

The most famous Indo-South African dish is bunny chow, a meat curry served in a hollowed-out loaf of Western-style bread. One explanation of its name is that in Durban Indian merchants were often called *banias*, the name of a caste of traders. They opened small restaurants that blacks could not enter because of apartheid but where they could (illegally) be served at the back door. An enterprising restaurant owner got the idea of hollowing out a small loaf of bread, pouring in curry, topping it with Indian pickles and handing it over to the customer without cutlery. The dish was named bunny chow, from 'bania chow'.

Under apartheid, Cape Malay food was rarely served in mainstream hotels and restaurants but it was available in Malay 'cook shops' specializing in *kerriekerrie* on Cape Town's side streets. Today, fortunately, there is no shortage of South African restaurants serving traditional Cape cuisine.

Other African Countries

Indian, and later Arab merchants came to East Africa for cloves, nutmeg, cinnamon and pepper. The North African traveller Ibn Battuta, who visited Mogadishu (now in Somalia) in 1331, describes a dinner that sounds much like a modern Indian meal:

> Their food is rice cooked with ghee placed on a large wooden dish. They put on top dishes of *kushan* – this is the relish, of chicken and meat and fish and vegetables. They cook banana before it is ripe in fresh milk and they put it on a dish, and they put sour milk in a dish with pickled lemon on it and bunches of pickled chilies, vinegared and salted, and green ginger and mangoes . . .

Ugali is Swahili for a porridge-like dish made from corn meal that is a staple in southern and eastern Africa. It is rolled into a ball and dipped in a meat, vegetable or fish curry.

> When they eat a ball of rice, they eat after it something of these salted and vinegared foods . . . Now one of these people of Maqdashaw habitually eats as much as a group of us [Moroccans] would. They are extremely large and fat of body.[4]

The Portuguese established colonies in what are today Angola, Equatorial Guinea, Madagascar, Mozambique and Zanzibar. They introduced chillies, corn, tomatoes, sweet potatoes, cassava and the domestic pig from the New World; salt cod from Portugal; citrus fruits from their Asian colonies; and spices such as cloves, cinnamon and ginger from West Africa and India. Both the Portuguese and British brought Goans to their colonies as artisans and clerical workers. The Goan influence can be seen in the use of coconut milk as the gravy for many African dishes, especially those made with seafood.

A traditional meal in most of Africa is a thick porridge (made from boiled yam roots, plantains, corn, millet, sorghum or rice) eaten with a stew or sauce. The components vary by region but usually consist of oil, a vegetable and a small amount of protein (fish, meat, legumes, nuts). This pattern lends itself well to the adaptation of curry dishes. In East Africa, curry is typically made with chicken, goat or mutton and served with Indian-style bread or cornmeal (*ugali* in Swahili), pounded and boiled until it is very thick. Every household has a large tin of curry powder (*mchuzi*) on hand; chillies, called *peri peri* in Swahili, are grown everywhere. *Mchuzi*

Peri peri chillies are tiny super-hot chillies popular in many parts of Africa.

is also the name given to popular Zanzibar vegetable, meat, fish or seafood curry made with tomatoes, coconut milk, tamarind and curry powder and accompanied by bananas, pickles and either rice or chapattis (a bread that is popular in East Africa). Roast meat, called *nyama choma*, flavoured with curry powder, is another popular dish.

In 1888 the British established the Imperial British East Africa Company to develop trade in the region and later set up the Protectorate British East Africa, encompassing present-day Kenya and Uganda. Between 1896 and 1901, 30,000 labourers from India were recruited to build the Uganda Kenya railway. They were followed by other immigrants, mainly Gujaratis, who were moneylenders, traders and shop owners. By the mid-1960s, 360,000 people of Indian origin lived in East Africa, but most were forced to leave by new nationalist governments and emigrated to Britain and Canada. With regime changes in Uganda and Kenya, many have returned and today run grocery stores and small stands selling samosas, curry and other Indian dishes. Large cities like Mombasa and Kampala have many Indian restaurants.

Curries, called *carils*, are popular dishes in Mozambique and Angola, which were Portuguese colonies until the mid-1970s. According to Van der Post, Angolan curries tend to be 'either straightforward derivatives of the curries of India or pale imitations of those of South Africa, particularly Natal'. The Mozambican national dish is *peri peri* (also known as *pil-pil* and *pili-pili*), made by simmering freshly picked peri peri chillies in lemon juice, salting the mixture and pounding it into a paste, which is spread over meats, fish and shellfish. The dish spread to other parts of Africa and even to Portugal and Goa.

Curry powder and other spices are popular seasonings in Ethiopia and Eritrea, where stews (*wats*) eaten with the flatbread called *injera* are the national dish. The Ethiopian seasoning *berbere*, used in many dishes, can contain ginger, onion, garlic, cloves, cinnamon, nutmeg, cardamom pods, spice black pepper, fenugreek, coriander and very hot chillies. Curry powder is an ingredient in many dishes in West Africa, especially Nigeria, where it was brought by the British administrators in the colonial period.

6
South-east Asia

Mussaman curry is like a lover
As peppery and fragrant as the cumin seed
Its exciting allure arouses
I am urged to seek its source
King Rama II of Thailand,
Boat Songs, 1768–1824[1]

Overview

The countries of South-east Asia – Myanmar (previously Burma), Thailand, Laos, Vietnam, Malaysia, Cambodia and the island nations of Singapore, Brunei, East Timor, Indonesia and the Philippines – are plural societies characterized by a dominant ethnic majority and many minorities. From ancient times, the region held a key position in the trade routes between India and China and was subject to their political, cultural and culinary influences. Starting in the fourth century BC Indian merchants brought not only spices and textiles, but also Hinduism and Buddhism (the main religions of modern Thailand and Cambodia), new forms of dance, sculpture and music, and Indian concepts of statecraft. So-called 'Hinduized' kingdoms flourished in what are now Thailand, Vietnam, Cambodia and Indonesia until well into the eighteenth century.

These traders may also have introduced tamarind, garlic, shallots, ginger, turmeric and pepper to the region and disseminated herbs such as lemon grass and galangal (a ginger-like rhizome) from one area to another. The Chinese legacy includes such ingredients as soy sauce, tofu and bean sprouts and the technique of stir-frying.

In the eighth century, Arab traders took over the spice trade and converted many local people to Islam, today the dominant religion in Malaysia, Indonesia and Brunei. They introduced kabobs, biryanis, kormas and other meat dishes from the Islamic world (including the Delhi sultanate). They also popularized the use of cloves, nutmegs and other local spices. In 1511 the Portuguese established a trading post at Malacca on the Malay Peninsula and introduced the chilli, which was quickly assimilated as a replacement for white peppercorns.

In 1602 the Dutch East India Company (VOC) founded Batavia (modern-day Jakarta). It became the capital of the Dutch East Indies, the predecessor of modern Indonesia. The British acquired Penang Island in 1786, established Singapore in 1819 and later extended their control over the Malay Peninsula and Burma. They built pepper, sugar, tea, palm, coffee and rubber plantations and imported labourers from southern India.

The Spanish took control of the Philippines in 1571 and converted most of the population to Catholicism. The French lost most of their colonies in Canada and India to Britain in 1815, but developed a second empire between 1830 and 1870 when they moved into North Africa and parts of South-east Asia. By 1914 the French empire encompassed Indochina (Laos, Cambodia and Vietnam), Tunisia, Morocco, parts of West Africa and Madagascar. Thailand, known until 1939 as Siam, was the only South-east Asian country that was never colonized.

Throughout South-east Asia, rice is the staple (in many languages 'to eat' is expressed as 'to eat rice'), served with side dishes: grilled meat or fish; vegetables, soups and soup-like dishes; curry-like dishes with a thicker gravy; and condiments. The starting point for soups and curries is a paste of chillies, garlic, shallots or onions, galangal, aromatic leaves and herbs, and sometimes dried or whole spices. The paste (called *bumbu* in Indonesia, *rempah* in Malaysia) may include lemon grass, *makrut* (kaffir) lime leaves and zest, and basil leaves – ingredients rarely found in Indian cuisine. Aromatic spices (such as nutmeg, cloves and cinnamon) are used less frequently and then generally in meat-based dishes.

The spice pastes may be wet or dry, as simple as garlic, chillies and shallots or containing as many as twenty ingredients. They may be simmered with the curries or fried in oil or separated coconut milk. Coconut milk is the most common liquid; yogurt, a common thickener in Indian curries, is rarely used in the rest of Asia. Another standard ingredient is a cooked fish or shrimp paste (*kapi* in Thailand, *blacang* or *belachan* in Malaysia and Indonesia) and fish sauces, all made from fermented salted fish.

Thailand

Thailand has the most complex and sophisticated cuisine in South-east Asia. This reflects the continued presence of a royal court which encouraged the culinary arts, considerable regional diversity and a wide range of ingredients. The Theravada Buddhism practised by most Thais does not prohibit or even discourage the eating of meat except as a voluntary practice.

A traditional Thai meal includes rice, soup, salad, a steamed, fried, stir-fried or grilled dish, a spicy vegetable and fish dish, curry, condiments, dessert and fruit, served at the same time and in no particular order. Long-grain jasmine rice is preferred in southern and central Thailand, short-grain sticky rice in the north.

The Thai word for curry, *gaeng* (sometimes written *kang*, *gang* or *geng*), basically means 'any wet savoury dish enriched and thickened by a paste'. The starting point is an aromatic curry paste, either made at home or purchased. The ingredients for a curry paste are pounded together in a stone mortar, which allows the release of the essential oils that impart flavour and aroma. Preparing curry pastes can take half an hour for a daily meal.

Galangal, sometimes called wild ginger, is a component of many curry pastes in South East Asia.

Most Thai curry pastes contain shrimp paste (*kapi* or *gapi*) made from tiny plankton shrimp that are marinated in salt, dried in the sun, pulverized and fermented for months. The paste may be roasted on a banana leaf before using. *Kapi*, chillies, lime juice, ginger, garlic and palm sugar are combined to make one of the most typical (and ancient) Thai relishes, *nam prik*.

In addition to the basic ingredients, some Thai curry pastes contain *grachai* (wild ginger, similar to galangal), which has a slightly pungent flavour and is often used for decoration; coriander root, which imparts a sweet freshness; and lemon, Thai and holy basil, each with their distinctive nuances. The ideal is to achieve a balance of hot, sour, salty and sweet flavours in both an individual dish and a meal. As Thai food expert David Thompson writes:

> In a good Thai curry, each flavor should be tasted to its desired degree and no one flavor should overshadow another. The striving for a complex balance of ingredients is nowhere more apparent than in curries: robustly flavoured ingredients are melded and blended together into a harmonious, yet paradoxically subtle and cohesive whole.[2]

Curries are either water-based or coconut-milk-based. Coconut-milk-based curries are prevalent in Bangkok and central Thailand. Water-based curries are more common in northern Thailand on the border with Myanmar and Laos. These curries are hotter and sourer than in the rest of Thailand, because the dishes are not diluted with coconut milk or sugar. A popular dish is *Gaeng Hung Lay*, or Myanmar-style pork curry made with pickled garlic and black bean sauce. Noodles are eaten as lunch or a snack.

Thai curries are categorized by the colour of the paste used in their preparation. A red curry paste includes dried red chillies, peppercorns and lime zest, and sometimes roasted and ground 'Indian' spices such as coriander, cumin and cloves. This mixture is used with almost any kind of meat, fish or vegetable. Red curries have plenty of sauce which is salty sweet and can be quite 'fiery hot'.

Yellow curry paste, popular in fish and seafood stews, contains turmeric, ready-made curry powder and roasted coriander and cumin seeds. It is also the base of an Indian-like chicken curry called *geang garee* made with onions and potatoes, ingredients rarely used in Thai cuisine.

Green curry paste, combined with strongly flavoured meat or fish or bitter vegetables, contains fresh green chillies, basil leaves, lime leaves and often round green aubergines.

Panang/Penang curry paste is made with dried red chillies, white pepper and sometimes peanuts and is often used with

Thai curries, like this green curry, are categorized by the colour of the paste and ingredients used in their preparation.

beef dishes. Massaman/Mussamun curry, a thick stew-like curry made with lamb or beef, originated near the Malaysian border where there is a large Muslim population. The paste contains dried red chillies, ground coriander, cumin and cloves, white pepper, peanuts and, unusual for a Thai curry, roasted whole spices such as cinnamon, cardamom and nutmeg.

Thailand's Neighbours

The French brought in labourers from their colonies in southern India to their possessions in the region that is now Vietnam. One consequence is the use of southern Indian-style curry powders, especially in the south. Popular dishes are chicken curry (*cari ga*) made with coconut milk, and beef curry (*cari bo*) that often contains bay leaves, cinnamon, onions, carrots and potatoes or sweet potatoes. Dietary staples are long-grain Indian rice prepared with coconut milk cashews, ginger and onion, French baguettes or noodles.

Cambodian cooks use curry pastes called *kroeng* based on lemon grass, galangal, wild ginger, garlic, shallot, lime zest and turmeric. Like Thai curry pastes, they come in red, yellow and green versions. A Cambodian dish served on festive occasions is *samaran*, a thick rich beef or duck curry made with cardamom, ginger and ground peanuts. Dishes of lightly stir-fried leafy green vegetables and pickled vegetables balance the stews. Laotian curries are hybrids, using a herbal base similar to that used in Thailand, sometimes with fresh dill.

Myanmar, part of British India until 1948, is made up of many ethnic groups, but the two greatest influences on its cuisine are India and China. In the 1940s half of Yangon's (Rangoon's) population was of Indian origin; today Indians account for only 2 per cent. The Indian influence is apparent in

A Thai Massaman curry is Muslim in origin and generally made with beef. The curry paste usually contains turmeric, cardamom, cinnamon, cumin, cloves and nutmeg.

Myanmarese samosas, biryani, street-side snacks, breads and curries, which incorporate Indian spices and lemon grass, basil leaves and fish sauce. Curries made from freshwater fish are especially popular. The liquid can be fish stock, water or coconut milk.

Chickpea flour, toasted rice, garlic, onions, lemon grass, banana heart, fish paste, fish sauce and catfish cooked in a broth are combined to make the national dish, a Chinese-Indian-Myanmarese hybrid called *mohinga*, which is sold by streetside vendors. It is served with rice noodles, lime, crisp fried onions, coriander, spring onions and dried chillies.

Indonesia

The republic of Indonesia is an enormous country of nearly 15,000 islands; a population of 238 million, two-thirds of whom live on the island of Java; and a wide variety of languages, cultures and culinary practices. Although nutmeg, mace and cloves put Indonesia on the world stage, they appear sparingly in the cuisine (although cloves are a main

Throughout Myanmar, street-side vendors like this one in Mandalay sell dishes of *mohinga*, a fish noodle soup eaten for breakfast.

component of *kretek*, the local cigarette). The Dutch planted tomatoes, cabbage, cauliflower, carrots and other European vegetables in the highlands; the Indians brought cucumbers, aubergines and onions; and the Chinese introduced mustard greens, soybeans and soybean cakes.

According to Jennifer Brennan, there is really no haute cuisine in Indonesia.[3] Unlike in Thailand, the nobility reserved their creativity for literature and the arts. In much of Indonesia, boiled white rice is the focal point of a meal, supplemented by a soup, sautéed vegetables or *gado gado* (a salad of blanched vegetables in a peanut dressing), crunchy crackers (*krupuk*) made of flour, *perkedel*, corn or potato fritters, sometimes fried rice, a meat or fish stew, and at least one or several chilli-based fiery relishes called sambals that are widespread in Indonesia, Malaysia, Singapore, the southern Philippines, India and Sri Lanka.

Sambal goreng (literally 'fried relish') is a general term for an entire class of curry-like dishes made with meat, fish, seafood or vegetables. They may or may not contain coconut milk, and can be wet, dry or in between. In western Sumatra, a legacy of the ancient Indian and Arab traders is the use of such 'Indian' spices as coriander, cumin, turmeric and cinnamon. In Pedang, as well as the western and northern parts of the Malay Peninsula, a korma-like dish called *rendang* is popular. A traditional dish of West Sumatra, it probably arose from the need to preserve the meat from a newly killed buffalo as long as possible in the absence of refrigerators. A *rendang* is made by simmering pieces of beef or water buffalo in a gravy of coconut milk and a paste of garlic, chillies, ginger, turmeric and aromatic spices until it absorbs the liquid and turns nearly black.

Sambal bajak is an extremely hot Indonesian relish made with fried red chillies, tamarind juice, shrimp paste and ground nuts.

Nasi goreng is an Indonesian/Malaysian dish of fried rice prepared with egg, vegetables, shallots, soy sauce and chillies. It can be eaten by itself or served with meat or seafood.

The food of Java is more subtle, often combining sweet, sour and hot flavours. Main dishes include *sotos*, or soups; *sayurs*, thin stews with a preponderance of vegetables; and *gulais*, a word often translated as 'curry', made with a thickish coconut-milk gravy. Dutch-Indonesian hybrids include *kari jawa*, beef and potatoes cooked in coconut milk; *semur*, slices of beef served in a gravy made from sweet soy sauce, nutmeg and cloves, tamarind and palm sugar; and *pergedels* (from the Dutch *frikkadels*), deep-fried golden fritters made from seafood or vegetables. The Chinese influence is apparent in *nasi goreng* and *batni goreng*, fried rice or egg noodles with egg, vegetables, shallots, soy sauce and chillies, and served with fried chicken or shrimp, or a few sate sticks.

In some ways, the experience of the Dutch in the East Indies parallels that of the British in India. In the early days, employees of the Dutch East India Company, military officers and merchants often took wives and mistresses from the local population. These Javanese or Chinese women, called *Nonya* (sometimes written *Nona* or *Nonna*), were famous for their household management and culinary abilities. Cookbooks were written for them in Malay giving recipes for Dutch roasts, stew, waffles and pastries, Indian curries and Portuguese and Chinese dishes. (One of these authors, Nonna Cornelia, invented charming names for the women who contributed recipes: Mevrouw [Dutch for Mrs] Satay, Mama Cutlet, Ma-Kokkie Pork Chop, Nonna Fishy and Mevrouw Cucumber!) The first Dutch-language cookbook was published in Java in 1866.

Following the opening of the Suez Canal, more Dutch women came to the East Indies as wives. To help them adjust to their new lives, especially the entertaining required to maintain their husbands' social positions, a spate of magazines, household guides and cookbooks were published both in the East Indies and the Netherlands. A special training school was even opened in The Hague in 1920.

Familiarity with local culture and cuisine was considered important for Dutch administrators and a hybrid Dutch-Indonesian cuisine emerged. Its most famous product was *rijsttafel*, which translates as rice table, a meal composed of many small dishes of meat, vegetable, fish and condiments served with plain and coloured rice. Far from being authentic, it was invented in the late nineteenth century by Dutch planters in East Java (perhaps in imitation of a traditional Javanese ceremonial meal) as a way of showing off their affluence. Forty, sixty or as many as eighty male waiters, dressed in starched white uniforms with batik cummerbunds, would serve the corresponding number of dishes on silver trays. *Rijsttafel* was served in colonial homes as Sunday lunch, at dinner parties or even as a precursor to a European main course. It was standard fare on ships heading from the Netherlands to the East Indies as one way of acclimatizing new recruits. Today *Rijsttafel* is served in tourist hotels in Indonesia, on cruise ships and, in a truncated version, in restaurants in the Netherlands and former colonies such as South Africa and the Dutch Antilles.

Malaysia and Singapore

The Malaysian federation covers much of the Malay Peninsula and the north coast of the island of Borneo, which it shares with Indonesia and the kingdom of Brunei. About two-thirds of its 25 million-strong population are Malay, 25 per cent Chinese and around 8 per cent Indian, predominantly Tamils. Singapore, which seceded from Malaysia in 1965, has a large Chinese majority and Malay and Indian minorities.

Some Chinese came as traders as early as the sixteenth century; others were imported by the British to work in the tin mines in the early nineteenth century. The Indian workers, mainly Tamils from southern India and Sri Lanka, came as indentured labourers to work on the rubber and palm plantations. Indian civil servants trained in India also settled in Malaysia and Singapore.

The cuisine reflects this cultural diversity. While the various communities have retained their distinctive dishes, they have also produced some delicious hybrids that make Malaysia and Singapore an eater's paradise.

Malaysia has many dishes in common with Indonesia including satays, kormas, biryanis and *gulais*. In northern Malaysia, bordering on Thailand, the dishes and ingredients are closer to Thai cuisine. In the south-east, Javanese influences are apparent in the sour fish soups.

Many Chinese took Malay wives, called, as in Indonesia, *Nonya* or *Nyonya*, who developed the celebrated fusion cuisine called *Nonya* or *Peranakan*. It combines Chinese recipes and techniques with local ingredients such as coconut milk, galangal, candlenuts, pandanus leaves, tamarind juice, lemon grass, lime leaf and a strongly flavoured shrimp paste called *cincaluk*. No meal is complete without a *sambal belachan*, a side dish of fermented shrimp paste.

A well-known *Nonya* dish is curry chicken kapitan (no relation to country captain chicken; a kapitan was a prominent member of the community who served as an intermediary between the Chinese community and the Malaysian rulers). Pieces of chicken are sautéed in a spice paste containing anise, Indian spices, ginger, shrimp paste, garlic, shallots and chillies and simmered in a liquid of coconut milk, tamarind water and cinnamon stock and thickened with ground coconut.

Singapore, Kuala Lumpur and other Malaysian cities are famous for their street foods. The popular breakfast dish *laksa*, originally a *Nonya* recipe, is a fiery chilli-infused coconut milk broth containing noodles, *belachan*, prawns, lemon grass, shredded chicken, coriander and hard-boiled egg, always served with sambal and a slice of lime. A hot and sour *asam laksa* is made with tamarind juice and hot chillies; a milder *laksa lemak* uses coconut milk in the liquid. Another popular street food is fish-head curry, supposedly invented by two Indian cooks in Singapore in 1964. It incorporates southern Indian ingredients such as okra, aubergine, mustard seeds, fenugreek and curry leaves as well as the technique

Laksa, a fiery noodle and seafood soup served by street-side vendors in Singapore and Malaysia, is a product of the hybrid Malaysian-Chinese *Nonya* cuisine.

of 'tempering' – adding sautéed spices to a dish at the end of cooking.

South Indian curries, together with idlis, dosas, vadas, sambars and rasams, are served in Singapore and Malaysia's 'banana leaf' restaurants. A local equivalent of an Indian stuffed roti is *murtabak* (from the Arabic word for folded). A dough made from white flour is wrapped around spiced minced meat and beaten egg and folded into packets that are sautéed, cut into pieces and served with a curry sauce.

Singapore noodles, a standard item on North American and European Chinese restaurants, is not Singaporean at all but probably a creation of Cantonese restaurants in Hong Kong. This mixture of rice noodles, shrimp, pork, chicken, onions, red peppers and other vegetables flavoured with curry powder is similar to a Singaporean/Malaysian vermicelli noodle dish called *Xin Zhou Mee Fen* that is traditionally flavoured with ketchup and a little chilli sauce.

Although not an integral part of Chinese cuisine, curry powder is added to a few dishes in South China. Most Chinese cookbooks in the West contain recipes for chicken curry and curry-flavoured noodles. The curry powder sold in Chinese grocery stores is similar to Madras curry powder with the addition of star anise and cinnamon.

7
Other Regions

Give me *nasi goreng* with a fried egg
Some chilli sauce and some prawn crackers and
a good glass of beer to go with it
Wieteke van Dort, *Nasi Goreng*

There is scarcely a country in the world whose residents do not enjoy curry. The website www.indiandinner.com lists Indian restaurants and curry houses in more than 90 countries. Curries and Indian dishes are especially popular in Dubai, Doha and other Middle Eastern cities, while Indian and Pakistani restaurants in Saudi Arabia serve pilgrims during the Haj. There are even Indian restaurants in war-torn Kabul that cater to the large number of British and Indian expatriates. However, curry and curry-related dishes enjoy a special position in the former 'imperial heartlands', especially the Netherlands and Portugal, as well as in a country that had little connection with India or the mighty imperial powers – Japan.

The Netherlands' 350 years as a colonial power have left their mark on its cuisine. As one scholar writes, 'Dutch taste can broadly be described as having been formed by natives and immigrants . . . It may be viewed as one of the unforeseen consequences of the colonial era.'[1] Until the 1950s the main diet of the Dutch consisted of grains, tubers, meat, fish, cheese and butter. Eating was viewed as a necessity rather than as a pleasure; meals were 'austere, frugally spiced, and repetitive' and 'eating out' was enjoyed only by a small elite.

Although spices were available after the founding of the Dutch East India Company in 1602, they were mainly used by the rich. But after Indonesia won its independence in 1949, more than 200,000 people migrated to the Netherlands, many of them of mixed Dutch and Indonesian origin. Indo-Dutch women began making Indonesian meals in their homes, which were delivered by their husbands to their customers; later they opened small eateries. Indonesian cuisine also appealed to the 100,000 returning Dutch military personnel. An influx of Chinese immigrants opened restaurants serving quasi-Indonesian and Chinese dishes. Grocery shops called *tokos* opened to sell spices and other Asian ingredients.

In 1950 Dutch women's magazines began publishing recipes for Chinese and Indonesian dishes. The food industry produced sauces and seasonings for every conceivable dish, and farmers began growing vegetables once considered exotic. In the 1970s people of Dutch nationality started to arrive from Surinam, adding another note to the multicultural melody.

Today, The Hague, Amsterdam and other Dutch cities have many Indonesian restaurants, authentic or otherwise, as well as small establishments that serve a mixture of Surinam, Indonesian and Chinese food. A popular Surinam specialty is *roti kip*, a chicken curry served with potatoes, eggs, cabbage and Indian-style rotis.

Like Bollywood films, the Indian curries and spices on display in this Iraqi grocery store are popular throughout the Middle East.

Bamihap, a deep-fried snack of noodles coated in breadcrumbs, is served in snack bars and automats in Dutch cities

Snack bars and vending machines serve Indonesian-Chinese-Dutch fusion dishes, including *bamischijf* (a deep-fried snack of noodles in a breadcrumb crust), *nasi* balls (deep-fried rice balls with ketchup and sambal), *patat sate* (fries with satay sauce), *bami goreng* (fried noodles with seafood, meat, vegetables and sambal) and *loempia* (spring rolls). *Nasi goreng* (fried rice) has become a fixture of Dutch domestic cuisine and is sold in frozen or dehydrated versions in supermarkets. However, there is virtually no influence of Sri Lankan or South African cuisine.

The eating patterns of Portugal show traces of its far-flung global empire. Ginger, pepper, turmeric, coriander, cinnamon, fennel, cloves, allspice and chillies (especially the fiery peri-peris from Africa) are used to flavour some dishes, including *caldeiras*, a fish and vegetable stew. Dashes of curry powder (*caril*) are often added to stews and soups in even the remotest country kitchen. Lisbon has a few Goan/Indian restaurants, at least one of which, Sabores de Goa, serves such Goan specialities as *carils*, *chacuti*, *sorpatel*, and *xec xec*, a crab and coconut curry.

The French were less accepting of the foods of their south Asian empire than the British and the Dutch (perhaps because their own culinary tradition was so strong), and there are virtually no traces in their cuisine of their long association with India, which lasted until 1954.[2] The first Indian restaurant in France, Indira, was opened in Paris in 1975 by a member of an Indian government delegation. He was concerned about the absence of Indian restaurants in the city. Indian restaurants there are far outnumbered by establishments serving North African and Vietnamese food. The first published curry recipe was given by the pioneering restaurateur Antoine Beauvilliers in his *L'Art de cuisiner* (1814). At the University of Paris Exhibition of 1889, the composition of curry powder was established by government decree: 34 grams of tamarind, 44 grams of onion, 20 grams of coriander, 5 grams of chilli, 3 grams each of turmeric and fenugreek, 3 grams of cumin and 1 gram of mustard seed. These are typical components of a south Indian curry powder. Recipes for chicken curry (*cari de poulet*) in various editions of *Larousse gastronomique* are an almost surrealistic merger of elements of French, British and Indian cuisine. The onions are sautéed with ham, apples, garlic, thyme, bay leaves, cinnamon, cardamom and powdered mace. Curry powder is

A plaque marks the spot where Berliners claim that currywurst was invented in 1949.

Currywurst, grilled pork sausage sprinkled with curry powder and topped with tomato ketchup.

then simmered with tomatoes and almond or coconut milk and the dish is finished with a dollop of heavy cream.

In Germany, the most popular street and fast-food dish is *currywurst* – a finely grained pork sausage roasted on skewers with onions and green peppers, cut into bite-sized pieces, sprinkled with curry powder and topped with tomato ketchup. It is prepared *mit* or *ohne* – with or without skin – and *scharf* or *extra scharf* – hot or extra hot. It is usually served with fries topped with ketchup, mayonnaise or both. This dish may have originated in the Dutch *patat satay*.

Almost a billion currywursts are consumed in Germany every year, and a recent study indicated that eighty per cent of Germans consider the dish a central part of their diet. The dish is so dear to the German heart that a fight has emerged over its origins. Berliners claim that it was invented in 1949 by Herta Heuwer, owner of a snack bar the site of which is now marked with a plaque. But residents of Hamburg claim it was

Curry and rice is one of the most popular dishes in Japan and a favourite of Japanese schoolchildren.

first made in their city in 1947 by Lena Brucker, the central character in a 1993 novel by Uwe Timm, *Die Entdeckung der Currywurst* (The Discovery of Currywurst), which has since been made into a film.

Indian spices have been used in Scandinavian cuisine for hundreds of years, thanks to the region's thriving shipping trade. Curried herring or mackerel on toast is a popular dish.

Japan

In a survey conducted in the early 1980s, the Japanese named curry and rice (*kare raisu*[3]) as one of their favourite three home-cooked dishes (the others were pork cutlets and vegetable stir-fry), while Japanese schoolchildren voted it the best meal served for school lunch. In Japan, there is a saying that you are never more than five minutes away from a curry shop. (For authentic Indian food, you have to go to an *indo-ryori* restaurant.)

From 2001 to 2007 there was even a curry museum in Yokohama, a sort of curry theme park featuring hostesses wearing saris, exhibits on the history of curry and spices, and a food court that served an array of curries and dishes made with curry powder, including Okinawan curry made with sake, an omelette-rice curry, a curry cocktail and curry chocolate.

A Japanese curry is a distinctive dish. It consists of chunks of meat (usually chicken, beef and shrimp), carrots, onions and potatoes simmered in an ochre-coloured, curry-powder-flavoured, slightly sweetish sauce. The sweetness comes from apples or honey. Often a fried pork cutlet (*tonkatsu*) is placed on top. The rice and curry are served separately on a Western-style plate, to be mixed later, and are eaten with a spoon. Pickled vegetables or ginger, an essential component of a Japanese meal, are served on the side.

In many ways, curry is the antithesis of Japanese food, which is based on the principle that ingredients should retain their natural appearance and taste. Japanese food historian Elizabeth Andoh recalls her disgust at her first encounter with 'dreadful curry rice with a terrible smell which nauseated me'.[4] But there are many reasons for curry's popularity. Housewives like it because it is convenient, inexpensive and easy to make in microwave ovens. It is the Japanese version of comfort food with no pretensions to class or elegance. It is never served in upmarket restaurants, at parties or receptions, or to guests, but, as Japanese food expert Richard Hosking writes, 'Schoolboys love it and anyone planning a summer camp or a winter skiing holiday would be making a great mistake not to include it at least once on the menus.'[5] The spiciness of curry offers a welcome contrast to the blandness of traditional Japanese food.

Curry Man is the name of a popular American wrestler in Japan. He wears a plastic dish of curry as a helmet and his repertoire of moves includes the spice rack and the spicy drop.

The curry flavour comes from either powder or from a ready-made roux – a block of spices and flour suspended in animal fat. Scored for easy separation, these blocks range from mild to very hot. The most popular brands are S&B Foods Inc. (the name is a variation on C&B, standing for Crosse and Blackwell) and House Foods Corporation – multi-billion-dollar international companies founded in the 1920s. House Foods produced the first block of curry roux in 1960. A few years later it launched a line of roux with the odd name Vermont Curry (perhaps because it contains apples), a milder, sweeter version designed to appeal to children. The 1970s saw the creation of the hermetically sealed pouch that can hold foods without refrigeration and be reheated in boiling water. Today these bags account for 40 per cent of packaged curry sales. Unlike British curries, which sometimes use left-overs, Japanese curries are usually made from fresh meat.

Curry came to Japan in 1868 at the beginning of the Meiji Era (1868–1912), when Japanese ports were again opened to foreigners. (In the late sixteenth century, Portuguese traders and missionaries entered Japan and were sequestered for more than two hundred years in a small trading post near Nagasaki. They introduced stews, pastries, bread and fried foods such as tempura and cutlets.) Small communities of English merchants in Kobe and other cities brought manufactured curry powders. Articles in women's magazines and recipe books taught housewives how to make curry, and its popularity spread quickly. A Japanese cookbook, *Seiyo Ryori Tsu* (*The Western Cooking Expert*, 1872), describes a curry stew very similar to the curried chicken recipe in Mrs Beeton's cookbook of 1861.

There were several reasons why curry caught on in Japan. One was a fascination for all things Western during the Meiji and Tasho eras (1912–26). Curry belongs to a category of foods called *yoshoku*, Western dishes adapted to local tastes. These dishes also used ingredients such as potatoes, tomatoes, onions, eggs, chicken, beef, pork and butter that were not commonly used in Japanese cooking. The military wanted to

Japanese curry chains such as GoGo Curry have opened branches around the world. This menu from the New York restaurant offers special incentives for people who can eat super-hot dishes.

encourage meat consumption as a way of building up the physiques of Japanese youth and found curry-rice an ideal way to incorporate vegetables, rice and meat in one inexpensive substantial meal. The Emperor Meiji told everyone to start eating meat (which had been discouraged by Buddhism) and ate it himself.

Curry became a staple of menus of Japanese steamships travelling to Europe. In 1930 a merchant who had tried curry rice on board put it on the menu of the cafeteria in his department store in Osaka, where it became the best-selling dish. Curry houses were soon opened throughout the country. Today Japanese chains have branches in the United States such as Curry House, Coco Ichibanya and GoGo Curry. The Honolulu branch of Curry House features cheese, banana, hotdog, fried chicken and squid curries. They are available in seven levels of 'hotness' and with different quantities of rice up to a 1,300-gram serving that is free for anyone who can eat it in twenty minutes.

In 2007 GoGo Curry opened its first American branch in New York City. It is a kind of shrine to New York Yankees star Hideki Matsui. (*GoGo* means 55 in Japanese, Matsui's number when he played for the Yomiuri Giants.) The restaurant offers 55 cents off any entrée on days that Matsui hits a home run. Rice is served in five different-sized portions: walk, single, double, triple and grand slam.

A popular Japanese fast food is curry bread (*kare pan*): curry wrapped in a piece of dough dipped in breadcrumbs (*panko*) and deep fried. A character named *kare pan man*, whose head is made of curry bread, is one of the superheroes in *Anpanman*, one of the most popular Japanese anime cartoon series.

Curry is also a popular home-made dish in Korea. It is usually made Japanese-style from ready-made mixes.

8
Curry Today and Tomorrow

From its inception, curry was a product of globalization, spread throughout the world by merchants and traders, missionaries, colonial administrators and their wives, indentured labourers and immigrants. In the twenty-first century, curry remains the global dish par excellence as people move more freely between continents, and spices and other ingredients once considered exotic are standard items on supermarket shelves.

Curry's popularity is being enhanced by social and economic trends, especially in the developed world. One is a growing preference for spicier, 'hotter' food. This reflects not only consumers' greater sophistication and cosmopolitanism – Italian, Thai and Chinese meals, once considered ethnic and exotic, are now everyday fare in North America and the UK – but the exigencies of an ageing population. As baby boomers grow older, their senses of smell and taste deteriorate along with their eyesight and hearing, which means it takes more flavour to titillate their palates. Food experts have identified a preference for hot, spicy and bold flavours as one of the main consumer trends in the twenty-first century.

Health concerns also play a role. For thousands of years, spices have been used for prevention and cures in Indian,

Chinese and Indonesian systems of medicine. Today studies at leading medical centres are confirming the truth of this ancient wisdom. Of all the spices under investigation, the one that shows the most potential in preventing and curing diseases is turmeric, a key ingredient in curry powder. It holds the promise of slowing down or even curing many chronic maladies, ranging from indigestion and cold sores to diabetes, cancer, multiple sclerosis, arthritis, heart disease and Alzheimer's disease. Similar studies are under way for cinnamon, garlic, ginger and other spices.

Thus curry, the world's most global dish, promises to remain a centrepiece of the world's tables for many years to come.

Recipes

Historical Recipes

Abul Fazl's Ingredients for Dopiaza as served at Akbar's court (*c.* 1600)

— from Abu'l fazl 'allami, *The A'in-I Akbari*, trans. H. Blochman, 1989

10 seers* meat that is middling fat
2 seers ghee [clarified butter]
2 seers onions
¼ seer salt
seer fresh pepper
1 dam** each of cumin seed, coriander seed, cardamoms and cloves
2 dams pepper

*1 seer = 1 kg
**1 dam = *c.* 3 g

The King of Oudh's Curry

— from Emma Robert's edition of Maria Rundell's *A New System of Domestic Cookery*, 1842

Take half a pound of fresh butter, two large onions, a gill of good gravy (veal is best), one large pressed tablespoon of curry powder; add to these ingredients any kind of meat cut into pieces. Put the whole into a stewpan, cover it close, and gently simmer for two hours. When ready to serve up, squeeze as much lemon juice as will givc it an acid flavour.

Wyvern's Chicken Curry (The Platonic Ideal of an Anglo-Indian Chicken Curry)

— from *Culinary Jottings from Madras*, 1878

Cut a small chicken into pieces and dredge with a little flour. Make a cup of stock with the trimmings and bones, a sliced onion, carrot, pepper corns, celery, salt and sugar and another cup of coconut or almond milk.

In a stew pan, sauté six shallots or two small white onions cut into rings and a clove of finely minced garlic in two ounces of good quality tinned butter until yellow brown. Add a heaping tablespoon of the stock curry powder and one of the paste, or, if the latter is not available, two tablespoons of the powder. Cook for a minute or two, adding slowly a wineglassful of the coconut milk and then the broth. Simmer for a quarter of an hour to create a rich, thick, curry sauce. Keep the sauce warm while you prepare the chicken.

In a frying pan, fry a minced shallot in an ounce of butter or clarified beef suet for a couple of minutes, then lightly fry the chicken pieces. As soon as they are lightly coloured, place them in the gravy in the stew pan, marinating for at least half an hour. Then slowly simmer the mixture over a low fire, adding stock or water if needed to cover the chicken.

During this period, the bay leaf, chutney, and sweet acid should be added. If the paste was not added previously, pounded almond and coconut are now added with a little spice and grated green ginger. The curry should be tasted and more acid or sweet added if needed. As soon as the pieces are tender, a coffee cupful of coconut milk should be added and stirred for three minutes. If a dry curry is needed, the curry is simmered longer without the lid, but continually stirred so that the meat doesn't stick on the bottom.

Remove the seeds and juice from two or three tomatoes, chop them with a quarter of their bulk of white onion, and season the mixture with salt, two finely chopped green chillies, a bit of chopped celery, a pinch of black pepper, and a teaspoon of vinegar (preferably anchovy vinegar if available).

Dr Riddell's Country Captain Chicken

— from *Indian Domestic Economy and Receipt Book*, 1849

Cut a fowl in pieces; shred an onion small and fry it brown in butter; sprinkle the fowl with fine salt and curry powder and fry it brown; then put it into a stewpan with a pint of soup; stew it slowly down to a half and serve it with rice.

Mrs Beeton's Curried Mutton

— from *Mrs Beeton's Book of Household Management*, 1861

The remains of any joint of cold mutton
2 onions
¼ lb butter
2 dessertspoons curry powder
1 dessertspoon flour
¼ pint of stock of water

Slice the onions in thin rings and put them into a stewpan with the butter, and fry until a light brown; stir in the curry powder, flour and salt, and mix all well together.

Cut the meat into nice thin slices (if there is not sufficient to do this, it may be minced), and add it to the other ingredients; when well browned, add the stock of gravy and stew gently for about ½ hour. Serve in a dish with a border of boiled rice.

Eliza Acton's Bengal Currie

— from *Modern Cookery for Private Families*, 1845

6 large onions
2 oz. butter
1 clove of garlic
1 dessertspoonful of turmeric
1 tsp each of powdered ginger, salt and cayenne
½ cup of gravy
1½ lb of meat
Preparation time: 1 hour or more.

Slice and fry three large onions in the butter, and lift them out of the pan when done. Put into a stewpan three other large onions and a small clove of garlic which have been pounded together, and smoothly mixed with a dessertspoonful of the best pale turmeric, a teaspoonful of powdered ginger, one of salt, and one cayenne pepper; add to these the butter in which the onions were fired, and half a cupful of good gravy: let them stew for about ten minutes, taking care that they shall not burn. Next, stir to them the fried onions and half a pint of gravy; add a pound and a half of mutton, or of any meat, free from bone and fat, and simmer it gently for an hour, or more should it not then be perfectly tender.

Mary Randolph's Curry of Catfish

— from *The Virginia Housewife, or Methodical Cook*, 1838

Take the white channel catfish, cut off their heads, skin and clean them, cut them in pieces four inches long, put as many as will be sufficient for a dish into a stew pan with a quarter of water, two onions, and chopped parsley; let them stew gently till the water is reduced to half a pint, take the fish out and lay them on to a dish, cover them to keep them hot, rub a spoonful of butter into one of flour, add a large teaspoonful of curry powder, thicken the gravy with it, shake it over the fire a few minutes, and pour it over the fish; be careful to have the gravy smooth.

Thanksgiving Turkey Curry

— adapted from Daniel Santiagoe's recipe in *The Curry Cook's Assistant* and published in the *New York Times*, 25 November 1887

one chicken or the remains of the Thanksgiving bird
1 teaspoon yellow curry powder
1 tablespoon liquid butter
1 pinch of cayenne
one pint milk
spices, cinnamon and cloves
salt to taste
one large onion

Take a good stewpan and put the onion sliced and all the other ingredients except for chicken and cream. Mix well, place on the fire for five minutes or more, and then add the chicken cut in joints, and let simmer for a few minutes. Soon as meat is done it is ready for table.

When serving add one tablespoon of cream and few drops of vinegar for flavor. More milk or clear gravy can be added if the pint of milk is not sufficient to tender the meat.

Bobotee

— from Hildagonda Duckitt *Hilda's 'Where is it?' of Recipes*, 1897

2 pounds meat
2 onions
a large slice of white bread
1 cup milk
2 eggs
2 tablespoons of curry powder
a dessertspoon of sugar
juice of a lemon or 2 tablespoons of vinegar
6 or 8 almonds
lump of butter

Mince the meat, soak the bread in milk, and squeeze out dry. Fry the onions in a tablespoonful of butter (dripping will do). Mix all the ingredients – curry powder, sugar, salt, vinegar, etc., etc. – with the fried onion. Now mix all the meat and soaked bread. Mix one egg with the mixture, whisk the other with some milk, and pour over the whole, after being put into a buttered pie-dish or into little cups (the old Indian way), with a lemon or bay leaf stuck into each little cup. Put them in the oven to bake, and send to table in the cups or pie-dish. Serve with rice. (This dish is equally good made of cold mutton.)

Modern Recipes

Curried Goat, Trinidadian style

Ingredients

2 lbs / 900 g lean goat meat, cut into small pieces
1 teaspoon salt
½ cup / 200 g chopped onion
2 teaspoons minced garlic
3 teaspoons green seasoning*
½ teaspoon chilli powder
2 tablespoons vegetable oil
3–4 teaspoons Trinidadian curry powder

*Can be purchased at most food markets. To make one cup at home, take 3 tablespoons of chopped chives, 2 tablespoons each of parsley, thyme and shadow beni (or coriander leaves), 4 cloves of garlic and 2–3 tablespoons of water and grind in a food processor or blender until puréed.

Season the goat with the salt, onion, garlic, green seasoning and chilli powder. Heat the oil in a heavy pot. Mix the curry powder with 4 cups / 960 ml of water until it is a smooth paste, add to the hot oil and sauté for 2 minutes. Add the meat, coat with the paste and stir for around 10 minutes. Add 2 cups / 480 ml of hot water, bring to the boil, cover and simmer until the meat is tender.

Rendang Daging
(Beef Long-Cooked in Coconut Milk with Spices)

— from *Sri Owen's Indonesian Food* (London, 2008)

Ingredients

6 shallots, finely sliced
4 garlic cloves, sliced
1 in. / 2.5 cm piece of fresh ginger, peeled and roughly chopped
1 in. / 2.5 cm piece of turmeric root, peeled and roughly chopped or 1 teaspoon ground turmeric
6–10 fresh red chillies, deseeded, or 3 teaspoons chilli powder
1 teaspoon chopped galangal, or ½ teaspoon laos powder (ground galangal)
4 pints / 2.3 litres coconut milk
1 salam leaf or bay leaf
1 fresh turmeric leaf or 1 lemon grass stem
2 teaspoon salt
3 lbs / 1350 g buffalo meat or beef (preferably brisket; otherwise chuck steak or silverside), cut into ¾ in. / 2 cm cubes

Put the shallots, garlic, ginger, turmeric, chillies and galangal or laos powder in a blender with 4 tablespoons of the coconut milk, and purée until smooth. Put this paste and the remaining coconut milk in a large wok or saucepan. (It is generally more convenient to start in a pan and transfer to a wok later.) Add the meat and the rest of the ingredients, making sure that there is enough coconut milk to cover.

Stir the contents of the pan and start cooking, uncovered, over a medium heat. Let the pan bubble gently for 1½ to 2 hours, stirring from time to time. The coconut milk will by then be quite thick and, of course, much reduced.

If you started in a large saucepan, transfer everything to a wok and continue cooking in the same way for another 30 minutes, stirring occasionally. By now the coconut milk will have begun to reduce to oil and the meat, which has so far been boiling, will soon be frying. From now on, the rending needs to be stirred frequently. Taste, and add salt if necessary. When the coconut milk becomes thick and brown, stir continuously for about 15 minutes until the oil has been more or less completely absorbed by the meat. Take out and discard the salam or bay leaf, turmeric leaf or lemon grass. Serve hot with plenty of rice.

Malaysian Nonya-style Chicken Curry

— from Tourism Malaysia, *Flavours of Malaysia*

Ingredients

4–5 tablespoons oil
1 star anise
2 cloves
1 cinnamon stick
1 cup meat curry powder,* mixed with enough water to form a paste
1 cup / 200 ml thick coconut milk
a 3 lb / 1350 g chicken, cut into pieces
2 medium potatoes, peeled and cut into wedges
3 cups / 710 ml water
1 tablespoon salt
½ teaspoon sugar

**for the Meat Curry Powder*

1½ tablespoons each powdered coriander seed and cumin seed
¾ tablespoon powdered fennel seed
1 tablespoon chilli powder
½ teaspoon turmeric powder
1 teaspoon each of powdered cloves, cinnamon, nutmeg and cardamom

Heat the oil over a medium-low heat and sauté the spices. Add the curry paste and stir for several minutes. Add 2–3 tablespoons of the coconut milk if necessary to keep it from sticking and fry over a low heat until the oil separates. Add the chicken and fry for a minute. Add the potatoes and the water. Simmer until the chicken is tender and the potatoes are cooked.

Add the thick coconut milk and season to taste. Continue to cook until the gravy is slightly thick.

Guyanese Chicken Curry

— courtesy of Gaitri Pagrach-Chandra

Ingredients

1 medium onion
3 cloves garlic
3–4 tablespoons Caribbean or Madras curry powder
2 tablespoons garam masala
1 tablespoon ground coriander
1 teaspoon ground cumin
1–2 tablespoons cooking oil
1 lb / 450 g chicken breast, cut into small cubes
2 cups / 400 ml water or coconut milk

Grind the onion and garlic very finely in a small food processor. Mix the spice powders with enough water to make a paste, and let it stand for a while.

Heat the oil in a heavy pot. Sauté the onion paste until it has a slightly glassy appearance. Add the spice paste, stir until it starts to emit an aroma, then add the chicken and stir until it is well coated. When the mixture no longer appears glassy, pour in sufficient warm water or coconut milk to cover the chicken pieces. Cover and gently simmer for 20 to 30 minutes. Serve with white rice or roti.

Frikkadels

— courtesy of Paul van Reyk

Of old Dutch origin, these spicy meatballs are popular in South Africa and are an essential ingredient in the Sri Lankan dish *lamprais*.

Ingredients

1 lb / 450 g minced lamb or beef
1 slice dried bread, grated
1 tablespoon shallots, finely chopped
2 cloves garlic, finely chopped
2 thin slices ginger, finely chopped
1 teaspoon fennel or dill leaves, finely chopped
½ teaspoon ground cinnamon
½ teaspoon ground pepper
½ teaspoon grated nutmeg
½ lime, juiced
pinch of salt
2 eggs, well beaten in separate containers
breadcrumbs

Thoroughly mix the minced meat and all the ingredients except the second egg and the breadcrumbs together with your hands. Shape the mixture into balls the size of large marbles. Dip each ball in the remaining beaten egg and roll it in the breadcrumbs until crusted over. Deep-fry until golden-brown. A good way to know when to take them out is when the bubbles they release have reduced to a trickle.

Thai Mussamun Beef Curry

Ingredients

2 tablespoons oil
1½ teaspoons Mussamun curry paste

1 lb / 450 g stewing beef, cut into cubes
2 medium potatoes, cut into 1 in. / 2.5 cm cubes
1 onion, cut into four pieces
1½ cups coconut milk
1–2 tablespoons fish sauce, to taste
1 teaspoon sugar
1–5 chopped red chilli peppers, to taste
½ cup roasted peanuts

Heat the oil in a heavy pot or wok and sauté the curry paste until it bubbles. Add all the other ingredients except the peanuts, stir well, bring to the boil, reduce the heat and simmer for 45 minutes to an hour until the meat is tender. Sprinkle with the peanuts and serve with white rice.

Fijian Tinned Fish Curry

2 minced cloves of garlic
1 in. / 2.5 cm grated fresh ginger
½ teaspoon cumin seed
1 teaspoon mustard seed
1 medium onion, grated
½ teaspoon turmeric
1 tablespoon tomato paste
16 oz/500g tinned tuna or mackerel
red chillies to taste
1 cup / 150 g frozen peas
1 teaspoon garam masala

Heat the oil from one of the tins of tuna and sauté the garlic, ginger, cumin and mustard seed until the mustard seed starts to pop. Add the onion and fry until soft. Add water or more oil if needed to prevent sticking. Add the turmeric and tomato paste and stir until it forms a paste. Add the fish, chillies, peas and garam masala and cook until heated through. Serve with roti or rice.

References

Introduction

1 Patak's Indian Foods has received orders from curry-deprived British scientists studying penguins in the Antarctic. Shops in St John's, Newfoundland, stock Indian spices. Beijing has more than forty Indian restaurants, while in Warsaw a curry club meets monthly to sample curry in that city's restaurants.

2 A survey of eleven curry powders sold in the UK and the US found that all contained cumin, fenugreek and turmeric; ten also included coriander seeds. The next most popular ingredients were cloves, fennel seeds and ginger (found in seven powders); garlic and red pepper (six); black pepper (five); curry leaves, cardamom, cinnamon, nutmeg and white pepper (four); chillies, mustard seed and poppy seed (two); and anise, Bengal gram, cassia buds, celery seeds, dill seeds, mace, onion and triphala (a herb used in Ayurvedic medicine, one). The Madras curry powders surveyed did not contain 'warm' or 'aromatic' spices such as cardamom, cloves and nutmeg and usually included curry leaves and chillies.

3 One being that a Scotsman in Bombay named Curry liked food made with chillies so much that the dishes were named after him; another that the word curry comes from *cuirreach gosht*, which means racetrack meal in Irish, so named

because an Irish sea captain gambled away his wife's fortune, forcing the family to sell some horses and eat the rest.

4 Pietro Della Valle, *The Travels of Pietra Della Valle in India, from the old English Translation of 1664*, cited in David Burnett and Helen Saberi, *The Road to Vindaloo: Curry Books and Curry Cooks* (Totnes, 2008), p. 12.

1 The Origins of Curry

1 The Indian subcontinent also comprises Pakistan, Bangladesh, Bhutan, Nepal and the island of Sri Lanka, which were once part of British India. In this book, India refers to the entire region. Political boundaries are rarely commensurate with linguistic or gastronomical borders, and there is no clear demarcation line between the food of India and its neighbours.

2 Iqitdar Husain Siddiqi, 'Food Dishes and the Catering Profession in Pre-Mughal India', *Islamic Culture*, LIV/2 [Hyderabad] (April 1985), pp. 117–74.

3 K. T. Achaya, *Indian Food: A Historical Companion* (New Delhi, 1994), p. 154.

4 Emma Roberts, *Scenes and Characteristics of Hindoostan, with Sketches of Anglo-Indian Society*, 2nd edn (London, 1837), vol. I, p. 75.

5 Lizzie Collingham, *Curry: A Tale of Cooks and Conquerors* (Oxford, 2006), pp. 115–16.

2 Britain

1 Quoted in Jo Monroe, *Star of India: The Spicy Adventures of Curry* (Chicester, 2004), p. 136. However, a 1998 survey found that curry was only the sixth most popular dish behind fish and chips, steak and chips, chicken, lasagne and roast dinner.

2 Anon., *Modern Domestic Cookery* (London, 1851), p. 311,

quoted in Susan Zlotnick, 'Domesticating Imperialism: Curry and Cookbooks in Victorian England', *Frontiers: A Journal of Women's Studies*, XVI/2–3, p. 5.

3 F. W. Moorman, *Songs of the Ridings* (London, 1918) on alt-usage-english.org/ucle/Moorman

4 'Curry', in *The Humorous Poetry of the English Language*, ed. James Parton (New York, 1857), pp. 474–5. Quoted in Zlotnick, *Domesticating Imperialism*, p. 10.

5 This was one of a series of exhibitions that began with the Great Exhibition of 1851 in the Crystal Palace. The Empire of India Exhibition in Earls Court, 1895–6, featured a replica of an Indian town, a Moghul garden, snake charmers and a curry house.

6 E. P. Veeraswamy, *Indian Cookery* (Mumbai, 2001), pp. 9–11.

3 The Colonies: The United States, Canada and Australia

1 Molly O'Neill, 'Long Ago Smitten, She Remains True to the Country Captain', *New York Times*, 17 April 1991; Sam Sifton, 'Master Class', *The New York Times Magazine*, 25 January 2009, pp. 47–8.

2 Jane Holt, 'News of Food', *New York Times*, 16 January 1941.

3 Craig Claiborne, 'Dining at the Fair', *New York Times*, 27 June 1964.

4 Quoted in Craig Claiborne, 'As an Indian Cook Tells it, Curry Powder is the Villain', *New York Times*, 30 May 1974.

5 The historical information and quotations in this section come from the excellent article by Mary F. Williamson, 'Curry: A Pioneer Canadian Dish', *Multiculturalism*, 1979 II/3, pp. 21–4.

6 Quoted in Barbara Santich, *In the Land of the Magic Pudding: A Gastronomic Miscellany* (Kent Town, 2000), p. 80.

7 Danny Katz, 'The Culinary Revolution that Just Won't Quit', 20 March 2005, theage.com.au.

5 Africa

1 Indians, mainly from Bengal and the Malabar and Coromandel coasts, accounted for 36 per cent of the early slaves, compared with 31.5 per cent from Indonesia and 37 per cent from Africa, mainly Guinea and Madagascar. Frank R. Bradlow and Margaret Cairns, *The Early Cape Muslims: A Study of their Mosques, Genealogy and Origins* (Cape Town, 1978), p. 102. Other Indians were captured and taken by the Dutch to Indonesia as slaves.

2 Hilda Gerber, *Traditional Cookery of the Cape Malays* (Amsterdam and Cape Town, 1957), p. 10.

3 Laurens Van der Post, *African Cooking* (New York, 1970), p. 136.

4 Said Hamdun and Noël King, *Ibn Battuta in Black Africa* (Princeton, 1994), cited on congocookbook.com.

6 South-east Asia

1 Quoted in David Thompson, *Thai Food* (Berkeley, CA, 2002), p. 24.

2 Ibid., p. 275.

3 Jennifer Brennan, *The Cuisines of Asia* (New York, 1984), p. 36.

7 Other Regions

1 Anneke H. Van Otterloo, 'Chinese and Indonesian Restaurants and the Taste for Exotic Food in the Netherlands: A Global-local Trend', *Asian Food: The Global and the Local*, ed. Katarzyna Cwiertka with B. Walraven, (Honolulu, 2001), pp 153–66.

2 Today French butchers still flavour their pâtés with *quatres épices* made from pepper, cloves, ginger and nutmeg – a legacy of the sixteenth and seventeenth centuries when spice use was fashionable.

3 The normal Japanese word for cooked rice is *gohan*, which is used only when rice is eaten with chopsticks from a bowl.

4 Quoted in Keiko Ohnuma, 'Curry Rice: Gaijin Gold: How the British Version of an Indian Dish Turned Japanese', *Petits Propos Culinaires*, VIII (1966), p. 8.

5 Richard F. Hosking, 'India–Britain–Japan: Curry-Rice and Worcester Sauce', *Hiroshima Shudo University Research Review*, VIII (1992).

Select Bibliography

Achaya, K. T., *Indian Food: A Historical Companion* (New Delhi, 1998)

—, *A Historical Dictionary of Indian Food* (New Delhi, 2002)

Brennan, Jennifer, *The Cuisines of Asia* (New York, 1984)

—, *Curries and Bugles* (London, 1992)

Brissenden, Rosemary, *Southeast Asian Food* (Singapore, 2007)

Burnett, David, and Helen Saberi, *The Road to Vindaloo: Curry Books and Curry Cooks* (Totnes, 2008)

Burton, David, *The Raj at Table* (London, 1993)

Chapman, Pat, *The New Curry Bible* (London, 2004)

Chaudhuri, Nupur, 'Shawls, Jewelry, Curry and Rice in Victorian Britain', in Nupur Chaudhuri and Margaret Strobel, *Western Women and Imperialism* (Bloomington, IN, 1992)

Collingham, Lizzie, *Curry: A Tale of Cooks and Conquerors* (New York, 2006)

Davidson, Alan, *The Oxford Companion to Food* (Oxford, 1999)

Jaffrey, Madhur, *Madhur Jaffrey's Ultimate Curry Bible* (London, 2003)

Monroe, Jo, *Star of India: The Spicy Adventures of Curry* (Chichester, 2004)

Osseo-Asare, Fran, *Food Culture in Sub-Saharan Africa* (Greenwood, CT, 2005)

Pagrach-Chandra, Gaitri, 'Damra Bound: Indian Echoes in Guyanese Foodways', *Food and Memory: Proceedings of the Oxford Symposium on Food and Cookery, 2000* (Totnes, 2001)

Panayi, Panikos, *Spicing Up Britain: The Multicultural History of British Food* (London, 2008)
Patel, Sonja, *The Curry Companion* (London, 2006)
Trang, Corinne, ed., *Curry Cuisine: Fragrant Dishes from India, Thailand, Vietnam and Indonesia* (New York, 2006)
Van der Post, Laurens, *African Cooking* (New York, 1970)
Van Esterik, Penny, *Food Culture in Southeast Asia* (Westport, CN, 2008)
Veeraswamy, E. P., *Indian Cookery* (Mumbai, 2001)
Williamson, Mary F., 'Curry: A Pioneer Canadian Dish', *Multiculturalism*, II/3, (1979), pp. 21–4

Websites and Associations

Recipes and news about the UK curry scene

curryhouse.co.uk
The Curry Club (UK): patchapman.co.uk

General recipes

epicurious.com;
curry-recipes.info;
recipes4us.co.uk

Thai curries

templeofthai.com/cooking

Indonesian food

sriowen.com

African recipes

africa.upenn.edu/Cookbook/about_cb_wh.html

Historical curry recipes

digital.lib.msu.edu/projects/cookbooks

Acknowledgements

Writing this book proved more difficult than I had anticipated because so many excellent books and articles have appeared in recent years, especially about curry in Great Britain. In this little book, I've looked at curry's incarnations not only in Britain and its former colonies, but also in other parts of the world, including the former colonial outposts of the Portuguese and Dutch empires.

Many people helped me in this endeavour. I'd like to thank Andy Smith for asking me to write this book; my Australian colleagues Rachel Ankeny Gae Pincus, Barbara Santich, Michael Symons and Paul van Rejk for their helpful suggestions and, in Paul's case, a recipe; Richard Hosking, as always, a source of invaluable information about Japanese food; Tara Misir Sharma, Indu Sharma and Estella Lalgee for sharing their experience of Trinidadian food; Mary Williamson for her insights into curry in Canada; Marieke van Damme of the Boston Historical Society for providing information about curry in early Boston taverns; and Sri Owen for permission to use one of her recipes. Gaitri Pagach-Chandra very generously supplied a recipe, translations of Dutch songs and information about colonial food in the Netherlands and Guyana. Bruce Kraig offered much helpful advice. Stephen Bishop, Sunil Khushal, Jayashree Mazumdar Hart, Karen Leonard and Ashoka Bajaj provided invaluable assistance in my search for illustrations. I am especially grateful to my friend Helen Saberi for her encouraging and perceptive comments (always tactfully made) and my husband Ashish for his many suggestions and constant support.

Photo Acknowledgements

The author and publishers wish to express their thanks to the below sources of illustrative material and/or permission to reproduce it. Locations of some artworks are also given below.

British Library: p. 19; Rebekah Burgess/Bigstockphoto: p. 72; Cartoon-stock: p. 50; Shariff Che'Lah/Bigstockphoto: p. 93; Vivian Constantinopoulos: p. 61; Leena Damle/Bigstockphoto: p. 9; Bruno Ehrs/Corbis: p. 18; FabFoodPix/Food Collection/Stockfood: p.82; Martin Garnham/Bigstockphoto: p. 87; Courtesy of *GoGo Curry Restaurant*, New York, NY: p. 115; Joe Gough/Istockphoto: pp. 6, 49; Alexander Heitkamp/Bigstockphoto: p. 8; Aimee Holman/Bigstockphoto: p. 75; India Office/British Library: p. 21; Chan Pak Kei/Istockphoto: p. 112; Kumar Mahabir, *Caribbean East Indian Recipes*, 1992: p. 70; Michael Leaman/Reaktion Books: pp. 22, 23, 25, 28, 66, 78; Karen Leonard, *Making Ethnic Choices: California's Punjabi-Mexican Americans*: p. 59; National Library of Australia: p. 65; Yong Hian Lim/Bigstockphoto: p. 104; Linda & Colin McKie/Istockphoto: p. 12; Arild Molstad/Rex Features: p. 108; Brett Mulcahy/Bigstockphoto: p. 32; Museum of London: p. 44; Robert Opie: pp. 11, 41; Colleen Sen: p. 55; Rohit Seth/Bigstockphoto: p. 71; Bhupendra Singh/Bigstockphoto: p.10; Mark Skipper: p. 86; *Taj Mahal Restaurant*, Centurion, South Africa: p. 84; Khen Guan Toh/Bigstockphoto: p. 95; Andreas Weber/Bigstockphoto: p. 111; Anke van Wyk/Bigstockphoto: p. 83.

Index

italic numbers refer to illustrations; **bold** to recipes